Harvey Penick's Little Red Book

LESSONS AND TEACHINGS FROM A LIFETIME IN GOLF

Harvey Penick
with Bud Shrake

SIMON & SCHUSTER
New York   London   Toronto   Sydney   Tokyo   Singapore

SIMON & SCHUSTER
Simon & Schuster Building
Rockefeller Center
1230 Avenue of the Americas
New York, New York 10020

Copyright © 1992 by Harvey Penick and Bud Shrake, and
Helen Penick

All rights reserved
including the right of reproduction
in whole or in part in any form.

SIMON & SCHUSTER and colophon are registered trademarks
of Simon & Schuster Inc.

Manufactured in the United States of America

31 33 35 37 39 40 38 36 34 32

Library of Congress Cataloging in Publication Data
Penick, Harvey.
  [Little red book]
  Harvey Penick's little red book: lessons and teachings from a lifetime in golf/Harvey Penick with Bud Shrake.
    p. cm.
  1. Golf. 2. Golf—United States—Anecdotes. I. Shrake, Edwin.
II. Title.
GV965.P415   1992
796.352—dc20   92-202
                                                           CIP

ISBN: 0-671-75992-2

Simon & Schuster books may be purchased for educational, business, or sales promotional use. For information please write to:

Vice President of Special Markets
Special Markets Department
Simon & Schuster
15 Columbus Circle
New York, NY 10023

This book is written not only to help all golfers with their own games but to help club pros and teachers with their teaching.

—HARVEY PENICK,
Austin Country Club,
Austin, Texas,
1992

Contents

Introductions	11
My Little Red Book	21
Golf Medicine	27
What's the Problem	27
Looking Up	28
Hand Position	28
The Three Most Important Clubs	29
The Grip	30
The Waggle	34
Holding the Club	35
The Easiest Lesson	36
Palm Reading	37
Starting Young	38
Hole Them All	40
Learning Around the Cup	41
Do You Need Help?	43
The Right Elbow	44
Take Dead Aim	45
Beware	46
How to Knock Five Strokes Off Your Game	47
Reassurance	50
The Practice Swing	51
The Average Golfer	53

How to Tell Where You're Aimed	54
Seasoned Citizens	55
The Left Heel	60
Backspin	61
Heavy Clubs	62
Hints on Greenskeeping	63
The Wrist Cock	65
Hit a Full Approach	66
Easy Bunkers	67
Bunker Play	69
Don't Relax	70
Positive Thinking	71
Psychology	73
Stay Behind the Ball	75
Hitting From the Top	77
Hypnotism	80
The Slow-Motion Drill	81
Powder the Ball	82
Ball Position	83
Swing the Bucket	84
The Weed Cutter	85
Placing Your Feet	86
The Turn	87
Instant Humility	88
Maxims	89
The Mythical Perfect Swing	92
First Things First	93
The Prettiest Swing	94
Hitting the Target	95

The Magic Move	96
How to Practice the Full Swing	97
Warming Up in a Hurry	99
Chipping	100
Putting	101
The Dreaded Four-Footer	105
The Shank Shot	108
Why I Decided to Become a Teacher	109
The Stance	110
A Very Bad Habit	111
The First-Time Student	112
Competition	113
Kids and Carts	115
A Story by Helen	116
Learning	117
Some of the Women in My Life	118
And Some of the Men in My Life	129
The Sexes	140
A Practice Rule	141
John Bredmus	142
Hooking and Slicing	148
Strange Penalty	149
Yardage	150
Long and Short	151
Best Dressed	152
My Best Boys	153
Chip or Pitch	154
Out of Sight	155
The Follow-through	156

A Little Bit	157
A Golfer's Poem	159
Preparing for a Big Match	161
Uphill and Downhill	162
Playing in the Wind	163
Titanic Thompson	164
Trick Shots	167
Caddies	170
A Life in Golf	172

Introductions

by Tom Kite

WHETHER OR NOT you realize it, you are about to read one of the most important golf instruction books ever written, if not *the* most important. If you have never had the opportunity to take a lesson from Harvey Penick, that statement may surprise you some. But even better is the fact that this lesson will be enjoyable and you will learn something that should improve your game.

This is the effect that "Mr. Penick's son," Harvey, has had on his students for many a decade. No one can help but enjoy being around Harvey. He is as comfortable as an old pair of jeans, as unpretentious as a young child, and yet is one of the smartest men I have ever had the pleasure to meet. No, not book smart, but people smart. He truly knows, understands and loves people. And people truly enjoy being around him. As a matter of fact, some of my favorite memories are the rainy winter days when no one was on the course and we could all gather around Harvey and try to get inside his mind.

Harvey has often said that one of the things that has helped him become a better teacher is the fact that he has probably seen more golf balls hit by more students than anyone else. But there are lots of teachers who have spent countless hours on the practice tee with students, with little in the way of results to show for it. Harvey's students always improve, and at the same time Harvey improves as a teacher. Even at this stage in his career, he says he learns something new about golf every day. Contrast that to one of today's method teachers who says there is only one way to swing the club. Harvey allows the swing to fit the student—his or her personality. What other reason could there be for the tremendous numbers of great players who have worked with Harvey while most teachers are lucky if they ever have one? There are so many tour players who have come to Austin for a checkup that any list is bound to omit some. But Mickey Wright, Betsy Rawls, Sandra Palmer, Judy Kimball, Kathy Whitworth, Terry Dill, and Don and Rik Massengale probably made the trip more than most. No less than Bob Toski once commented that only Harvey Penick could have produced two players with such different personalities and athletic abilities as Ben Crenshaw and me without stifling one while helping the other achieve greatness.

But he is not only a pro's teacher. Harvey still gets goose bumps watching a beginning student get a ball into the air for the first time or teaching a 21-handicapper to get out of a trap. For years I would have put the Austin C. C. up against any club in the nation for the number of single-digit handicappers, because if a student had some time, he or she almost had to improve with Harvey as tutor.

But don't be misled into thinking that Harvey taught us all the same thing or even the same way. I have never seen him give a group lesson. To the contrary, he would shoo away any sideline watchers for fear they would overhear something that didn't apply to their games. In over thirty years of playing golf with Ben Crenshaw, I have never been allowed to watch Ben take a lesson from Harvey, nor has he been allowed to watch me. Harvey is so careful in choosing what he says that I have often seen him fail to respond to a question until the next day for fear that his answer would be misconstrued. And I can assure you that every answer he finally did come up with was always, always expressed in a positive way. Never would Harvey say "don't do that," but "could we try a little of this?"

But when it is all said and done, when the drives no longer have the carry they used to, when the iron shots are not as crisp as they once were, and the 29 putts per round are now more like 33 or 34, the one thing that we all have learned from Harvey is love. A love of a game that teaches us more about ourselves than we sometimes care to know. And a love of the people that we share this game with. Harvey makes no distinction between the rank beginner who chops his way around the course or the touring pro with a swing as smooth as velvet. If a person loves the game, then Harvey will do anything in his power to try to help that person improve. And be assured his effect on his students is tremendous. As Dick Coop, the noted sports psychologist from the University of North Carolina, once said, "Harvey teaches in parables." I believe that Harvey must have had a good teacher too.

by Ben Crenshaw

A good friend of mine from west Texas remarked, after a lengthy conversation with me about Harvey Penick, "He seems to be the most *contented* man I have ever known." I thought that was a wonderful way to describe him. My friend, a fine player who played golf for the University of Texas, often thinks of Mr. Penick, and says that Harvey's teaching philosophy, as well as his simple outlooks on life, has helped him immensely to understand how we can, after all, make the most out of life. If we only knew how good we have had it under Harvey ...

Golf, in any form, has given Harvey contentment. Adding to Harvey's contentment is the fact that he knew what was to be his life's work at a fairly early age. I've often wondered when Harvey met Jack Burke, Sr., who was probably the first golf professional to have a substantial influence on the improvement of early Texas golf (in the 1920's). Harvey has told me a number of times of how often many future teachers would show up at the Burke household. Burke was from Philadelphia, and was most likely heavily influenced by the Scottish immigrant professionals on the Eastern Seaboard, who favored a no-nonsense fundamental approach to teaching. Of particular fascination to Harvey, I am sure, was Stewart Maiden's approach to teaching, mainly the handling of the young Bobby Jones in Atlanta. Maiden's words to his pupils were simple and direct, avoiding all technicality, which is one of Harvey's hallmarks. Harvey also said to me that the finest book of golf instruction for all is *Bobby Jones on Golf*, which contains Jones's own golfing genius as well as Maiden's, combined with miles and miles of common sense and Jones's beautiful command of the English language.

These men, along with so many other people interested in improving golf, were important in Harvey Penick's development, but what sets the great teachers apart from the others is not merely golf knowledge, but the essential art of communication. Very few teachers in golf have had it, as Harvey does, and I think that it would be safe to say that it requires a gift from Above. I know that Harvey has spent a considerable amount of his lifetime teaching golf, not thinking of *what* to say to a pupil, but *how* to say it. Harvey's messages always came across in soothing tones, for he always knew how fragile our psyches were when we were playing poorly. His mere choice of words suggested the direct antithesis of commanding tones.

For example, he would always inspect the hands of a pupil to check for calluses. If he found them, he might say, "Let's try and *place* our hands on the club." The inference is made thus not to "grab" or "twist" or "wrap" our hands around the club. "Placing" was always a valuable word since it implies lighter grip pressure. Therefore it became easier to swing the clubhead.

In many ways Harvey reminds me of Old Tom Morris. Old Tom was a fabulous golfer from St. Andrews, Scotland, a great player who won the British Open championship four times. Old Tom was not known for his teaching ability, as Harvey is, but rather for imparting his philosophies and the tradition of the game of golf to others in a way that stirred deep emotions. As Honorary Professional and Custodian of the Links at St. Andrews, he had seen many changes in the game, and this beloved character lived a long and prosperous life knowing that he contributed to others' enjoyment of the game, regardless of their level of achievement. Old Tom was wise, treated all men equally, and kept things very simple. It did not take much to make him happy. As long as he was around his many friends, and there was golf to be played and talked about, he was truly *contented.* Many times Old Tom would say "I've got mae God and mae gowff to see me thro'."

What a joy it will be for people who are serious about their game to read about Harvey Penick's life of helping others. The golf parts are easily understandable as they contain such a simple, common sense style. But those of us who are lucky enough to have been around him for a while have truly been touched by a man with unfailing courtesy and generosity, a special kindness the likes of which I have never before witnessed in any man. I have never, ever heard of him remotely raising his voice to another; he is truly a man filled with compassion for others. For all of his admirable traits, let us simply say that Harvey Penick represents the very best that life and golf can offer.

by Betsy Rawls

Harvey Penick was my only golf teacher for thirty years, until I retired from competitive golf in 1975. For me, Harvey reduced golf, as he did life, to a few sound, irrefutable, worthwhile principles. And he expressed those principles in simple unadorned, down-to-earth, and often humorous terms.

He was always a refuge from the complexities and emotional traumas of the tour. To come back and see Harvey was to become refreshed, to become inspired, and to be able to put things in perspective once more.

He always brought me back to the basic mechanics on which a good swing is built.

Harvey's strength of character, his morals, his dedication, and his great wisdom somehow made me a stronger and wiser person. To have had Harvey as a teacher, a mentor, and a friend has been one of the great blessings of my life.

by Mickey Wright

I had the pleasure of spending quite a few hours on the practice tee of the Austin Country Club with Harvey Penick, not only having him look at my swing but watching and listening to him.

I was always struck by the simplicity of his teaching. He insisted on a good grip as a prime determinant of the swing and tried to impart to his students the feel of a good swing through various devices he would have them swing, such as a scythe or a heavy ball on a chain.

He worked with his difficult students as individuals and didn't try to fit them into a mold. He stressed, appropriately, a good short game, and his outstanding students, like Ben Crenshaw, Tom Kite and Kathy Whitworth, were certainly outstanding in this area.

by Kathy Whitworth

Harvey Penick is not only the consummate club and teaching professional but a unique individual. He has never been interested in the financial rewards or the publicity that may have come his way. I personally do not remember ever paying for a lesson after the first few visits.

His biggest reward, he told me, was to help someone hit the ball better than they ever hit it before. His demeanor, his honesty, his integrity in how he lives his everyday life have probably had as much an impact on me as his teaching. To try to live up to his standards has been a wonderful experience and will be even more so since I am now trying to become a teaching professional myself.

Harvey has touched many lives through the years, and with this book and through the people who have had the privilege to know him, he will continue to touch many more. What a nice thought.

by Mary Lena Faulk

I believe Harvey Penick has helped more people swing better and enjoy the game more than anybody. I'm not just talking about great players (Betty Jameson, Betsy Rawls, Ben Crenshaw, to mention a few) but high handicappers as well. All who have taken a lesson from Harvey have come away with a greater knowledge and understanding of their problems and how to resolve them.

by Dave Marr

The world of golf is and has been full of very special people. It has been my good fortune to have met many of the people in golf, the good and the bad, over the forty-plus years I played the game. One of the very special people I've had the pleasure to know is Harvey Penick.

I've not met anyone more of a gentleman or anyone who gave more of himself to golf and its people. I believe he should be recognized for the character of the people he has touched all these many years.

If it's true that a teacher is judged by his pupils and what they accomplish, then Harvey Penick stands at the top of not just golf but golf as a way of life. I love Harvey Penick and all he has stood for all these years.

by Byron Nelson

Harvey Penick is one of the great teachers in the history of golf. He has helped many people with their games, including me and the hundreds of students I sent him.

Harvey is a fine gentleman who has become friends with most of his students. I will always consider him a good friend of mine.

My Little Red Book

AN OLD PRO told me that originality does not consist of saying what has never been said before; it consists of saying what you have to say that you know to be the truth.

More than sixty years ago, I began writing notes and observations in what I came to call my Little Red Book. Until recently I had never let anyone read my Little Red Book except my son, Tinsley. My wife, Helen, could have read it, of course, but a lifetime spent living with a grown-up caddie like me provided Helen with all the information about golf that she cares to know.

My intention was to pass my Little Red Book on to Tinsley, who is the head professional at Austin Country Club. Tinsley was named to that post in 1973, when I retired with the title of Head Professional Emeritus after holding the job for fifty years.

With the knowledge in this little book to use as a reference, it would be easier for Tinsley to make a good living teaching golf no matter what happens when I am gone.

Tinsley is a wonderful teacher on his own and has added insights to this book over the years. But there is only one copy of the red Scribbletex notebook that I wrote in. I kept it locked in my briefcase. Most of my club members and the players who came to me for help heard about my Little Red Book as it slowly grew into what is still a slender volume considering that all the important truths I have learned about golf are written in its pages.

Many asked to read the book. I wouldn't show it to Tommy Kite, Ben Crenshaw, Betsy Rawls, Kathy Whitworth, Betty Jameson, Sandra Palmer or any of the others, no matter how much I loved them.

What made my Little Red Book special was not that what was written in it had never been said before. It was that what it says about playing golf has stood the test of time.

I see things written about the golf swing that I can't believe will work except by accident. But whether it is for beginners, medium players, experts or children, anything I say in my book has been tried and tested with success.

One morning last spring I was sitting in my golf cart under the trees on the grass near the veranda at Austin Country Club. I was with my nurse, Penny, a patient young woman who drives us in my golf cart a few blocks from home to the club on days when I feel well enough for the journey.

I don't stay more than an hour or two on each visit, and I don't go more than three or four times a week because I don't want the members to think of me as a ghost that refuses to go away.

I don't want to cut into the teaching time of any of our fine club professionals, either. I can see Jackson Bradley out teaching on the practice line, and there are moments when I might want to make a suggestion, but I don't do it.

However, I can't refuse to help when my old friend Tommy Kite, the leading money winner in the history of the game, walks over to my golf cart and asks if I will watch him putt for a while. Tommy asks almost shyly, as if afraid I might not feel strong enough. His request makes my heart leap with joy.

I spend nights staring at the ceiling, thinking of what I have seen Tommy doing in tournaments on television, and praying that he will come see me. If Tommy wants, I will break my rule that I never visit the club on weekends, and will have Penny drive me to the putting green to meet with Tommy on Saturday and Sunday morning, as well as on Thursday and Friday. I know it exasperates Penny that I would rather watch Tommy putt than eat the lunch she has to force on me.

Or I may be sitting in my cart in the shade enjoying the spring breeze and the rolling greenery of our beautiful golf course, with the blue water of Lake Austin sparkling below, as good and peaceful a place as I know on this earth, and the young touring pro Cindy Figg-Currier may stop and say hello and eventually work up the nerve to ask if I will look at her putting stroke.

Certainly I will. I get as much pleasure out of helping a rising young pro like Cindy as I do a celebrated hero like Tommy.

Don Massengale of the Senior Tour had phoned me at home the night before for a long-distance putting lesson. I can't hear very well on the phone, and Helen had to interpret, shouting back and forth as I tried to straighten out Don's grip.

Earlier my old friend Ben Crenshaw, the Masters champion who had grown up with Tommy Kite in the group of boys that I taught at the old Austin Country Club across town, dropped by our home for a visit and brought his wife and daughter to see Helen and me. Ben is one of the greatest players of all time, a natural. When he was a boy I wouldn't let him practice too much for fear that he might find out how to do something wrong. Ben has his own course, designed by Ben and his partner, at the Barton Creek Country Club layout, a ten-minute drive away from us. It pleases me deeply when Ben drops by to sit on the couch or when he phones me from some tournament.

Ben hasn't been gone long before the doorbell rings and it's one of our members, Gil Kuykendall, who brings Air Force General Robin Olds into the living room and asks if I will give the general a lesson on the rug from my wheelchair. They are entered in a tournament, and the general has played golf only a few times. Can I teach him? In the living room? In half an hour?

General Olds is a jolly good fellow, thick through the chest. He was a football star at West Point. He has those big muscles that, as Bobby Jones said, can bend a bar but are no use in swinging a golf club.

I fit the general with a strong grip and teach him a very short swing. Just about waist high to waist high. This man is too muscle-bound to make a full swing, but he is strong enough to advance the ball decently with a short swing. He won't break 100 in the tournament, but he will make it around the golf course.

When the member and the general leave, Helen and Penny scold me. I am wearing myself out, they say. They remind me that before Ben dropped by, a girl who is hoping to make the University of Texas team had come to talk to me about her progress, and I had asked questions for an hour.

It's true that I have grown tired as the day became evening. But my mind is excited. My heart is thrilled. I have been teaching. Nothing has ever given me greater pleasure than teaching. I received as much joy from coaxing a first-time pupil, a woman from Paris, into hitting the ball into the air so that she could go back to France and play golf with her husband as I did from watching the development of all the fine players I have been lucky enough to know.

When one of my less talented pupils would, under my guidance, hit a first-class shot, I would say, "I hope that gives you as much pleasure as it does me." I would get goose pimples on my arms and a prickly feeling on my neck from the joy of being able to help.

Every time I found something about the swing or the stance or the mental approach that proved to be consistently successful, I wrote it down in my Little Red Book.

Occasionally I added impressions of champions I have known, from Walter Hagen and Bobby Jones to Ben Hogan, Byron Nelson and Sam Snead to Jack Nicklaus and Arnold Palmer to Kite and Crenshaw, as well as Rawls, Whitworth, Jameson, Mickey Wright, Sandra Palmer and many other distinguished players.

I prefer to teach with images, parables and metaphors that plant in the mind the seeds of shotmaking. These, too, went into the notebook—if they proved successful.

Many professional writers inquired during my long career as a teacher if they might write a book for me on how to play golf.

I always politely declined. For one thing, I never regarded myself as any kind of genius. I was a humble student and teacher of the game. What I was learning was not for the purpose of promoting myself in the public eye. I was never interested in money. What I was learning was to be shared only with my pupils, and ultimately the knowledge would belong to my son, Tinsley, and my daughter, Kathryn.

But on this soft spring morning that I mentioned earlier, with squirrels playing in the grass around the wheels of my cart, and a shiny black grackle prowling in the branches above me, I was sitting there wondering if I was being selfish.

Maybe it was wrong to hoard the knowledge I had accumulated. Maybe I had been granted these eighty-seven years of life and this wonderful career in order that I should pass on to everyone what I had learned. This gift had not been given me to keep secret.

A writer, Bud Shrake, who lives in the hills near the club, came to visit with me under the trees on this particular morning.

Penny gave Bud her seat in my cart. We chatted a few minutes about his brother, Bruce, who was one of my boys during the thirty-three years I was the golf coach at the University of Texas. Then it burst out of me.

"I want to show you something that nobody except Tinsley has ever read," I said.

I unlocked my briefcase and handed him my Little Red Book.

I asked if he might help me get it in shape to be published.

Bud went into the golf shop and brought Tinsley out to my cart.

I asked Tinsley if he thought we should share our book with a larger crowd than the two of us.

Tinsley had a big grin on his face.

"I've been waiting and hoping for you to say that," he said.

So that morning under the trees we opened my Little Red Book.

Golf Medicine

WHEN I ASK you to take an aspirin, please don't take the whole bottle.

In the golf swing a tiny change can make a huge difference. The natural inclination is to begin to overdo the tiny change that has brought success. So you exaggerate in an effort to improve even more, and soon you are lost and confused again.

Lessons are not to take the place of practice but to make practice worthwhile.

What's the Problem?

When teaching or learning what is wrong with a swing, first decide if the thing to work on is the swing itself or the angle of the clubface at impact.

Looking Up

LOOKING UP IS the biggest alibi ever invented to explain a terrible shot.

By the time you look up, you've already made the mistake that caused the bad shot.

When I tell a student to keep his eye on the ball, it is usually to give him something to think about that won't do any harm.

I've known only three or four top players who say they actually see the ball when they hit it. Even Ben Hogan told me he loses sight of the ball "somewhere in my downswing."

Hand Position

I like to see your hands toward the inside of your left thigh on every shot except the driver.

With the driver, I like to see your hands at your zipper. If this moves them slightly behind the ball at address, that is fine. It encourages hitting on the upswing.

The Three Most Important Clubs

HERBERT WARREN WIND, the stylish and learned golf writer, came to see me at the club and asked what I think are the three most important clubs in the bag, in order.

I said, "The putter, the driver and the wedge."

Herb said he'd asked Ben Hogan the same question. Ben had replied, "The driver, the putter and the wedge."

My reasoning is that you hit the driver 14 times in an ordinary round. But on the same day, you may have 23–25 putts that are outside the "gimme" range but within a makable distance.

A 5-foot putt counts one stroke, the same as a 270-yard drive, but the putt may be much more significant to your score.

Psychologically, the driver is very important. If you hit your tee ball well, it fills you with confidence. On the other hand, if you smash a couple of drives into the trees, your confidence can be shaken.

But nothing is more important psychologically than knocking putts into the hole. Sinking putts makes your confidence soar, and it devastates your opponent.

A good putter is a match for anyone. A bad putter is a match for no one.

The woods are full of long drivers.

The Grip

IF YOU HAVE a bad grip, you don't want a good swing.

With a bad grip you have to make unattractive adjustments in your swing to hit the ball squarely.

It's no good to make a beautiful Al Geiberger swing unless you grip the club like he does. If Al twisted his hands around into some kind of ugly grip and then made his graceful swing, he might knock the ball out of bounds.

I believe it is a nice idea to try to pattern your swing after that of a professional player who is close to your own height and body structure, but only if you also study and imitate that player's grip.

As a teacher I have learned that one of the most delicate matters to attend is the student's grip.

If the student comes to me as a once-a-week player who has been playing for years without improving, all I have to do is put his hands on the club in a good grip—and after the lesson I will never see him again. He will hit the ball so poorly that he will think I am the dumbest teacher in the country.

Changing a bad grip into a good grip requires a great amount of practice. Unless the student is willing and able to do this, I would indeed be a dumb teacher if I demanded a radical alteration from an ordinary player in one lesson.

But with a talented player who plays and practices

often, it can be a different, almost miraculous story.

Kirby Atwell was trying to make my team at the University of Texas. He had a good swing but a weak grip that caused an open club-face. His shots lacked authority and mostly flew off to the right of the target, except when he would try so hard to square the clubface that he would hit a nasty hook.

After I knew the boy and his game well enough, I moved his left hand to the right. Then I moved his right hand a bit more to the right, also.

Don't think that because you move your left hand you must automatically move the right to make it match. Often it's enough to move one hand and leave the other alone. But in this boy's case, he needed a stronger grip all around.

Kirby looked at his hands as I placed them on the club, and there was an expression of disbelief on his face.

"Harvey," he said, "if I hit the ball with this grip, I'll hook it over the fence."

I asked him to try.

He cracked a long, powerful shot that went as straight as a ball can go. He was astonished and delighted. Kirby became an excellent player at the University of Texas. But he had talent and the time and desire to take his new grip to the practice range and become confident with it before he took it to the golf course.

One grip does not fit all.

The interlocking grip, with the forefinger of the top hand laced between the little finger and the ring finger of the bottom hand, is for people who have short fingers. Gene Sarazen, Jack Nicklaus and Tom Kite use it.

The overlapping grip, with the little finger of the bottom hand wrapped into the hollow between the forefinger and middle finger of the top hand or on top of the left forefinger, is the most widely used among ordinary players as well as experts, though with many individual variations. Ben Hogan, Arnold Palmer, Byron Nelson, Ben Crenshaw, Sam Snead, Al Geiberger and Payne Stewart are just a few of the overlappers, and none of their grips are exactly alike.

The two-hand or ten-finger grip, with all the fingers on the handle—sometimes called the baseball grip (although the baseball bat is held more in the palms, and a golf club more in the fingers)—is especially good for women and older players who may lack strength, although some top professionals like Beth Daniel, Art Wall and Bob Rosburg have done well with it. Little Alice Ritzman adopted the ten-finger grip as my student and gained enough distance to play on the tour and become one of the longer drivers.

In his famous book, *Five Lessons,* written with Herb Wind, Hogan says the tips of the thumb and forefinger of the bottom hand should never touch each other. Others teach that the thumb and forefinger should meld like a trigger. Bobby Jones used the overlapping grip with the tip of his right forefinger not touching the handle at all. But the back of the first joint of his forefinger pressed against the handle. Victor East of Spalding built special grips with flat places for the back of Jones's right forefinger, which would be illegal today.

I can go on and on talking about the grip until it gets too deep for me to understand.

The fact is, a top player can change his grip enough to cause a draw or a fade, a slice or a hook, and an observer can't even see the change. The top player feels it, and it happens.

I happen to have long fingers, and long fingers feel good on a club in the overlapping grip.

If you will pick up a yardstick and let your hands fit it, that will come closer to giving you a good grip than anything I could write about where to point your V's and all of that.

Just pick up a yardstick and fit your hands to it and swing it.

Then put the same grip on a golf club.

There is one thing I like to see in common with all three grips. I don't want the left thumb straight down the top of the handle. I want the thumb a little bit to the right. Byron Nelson told me the left thumb position is one of the most important things I teach. The reason is that at the top of the backswing, that thumb wants to be underneath the club. This gives you control.

Coaching at the University of Texas, I encountered a lot of west Texas boys. West Texas boys were well known for their strong grips, which they develop because they play in the wind so often. They can hit a 7-iron so far you can't believe it. Off the tee they get great distances with a 3-wood or 4-wood, but they can't hit a driver. Their strong grips delofted the clubs so much that a driver face would be totally shut.

Billy Maxwell was the first west Texas boy I can remember who had what I would call a good grip, with his hands more on top of the club.

No matter which of the three grips you use, one fundamental is that the hands must be touching each other. They should be joined as one unit. They should feel like they are melted together.

The best thing to do is to find a grip that fits you and feels good and then stay with it.

If the ball is flying pretty well, your grip is all right.

If you keep fooling with your grip, you will find yourself making a mistake on your backswing to correct for your new grip and then making another mistake on your downswing to correct the mistake you made on your backswing.

As for your grip pressure, keep it light.

Arnold Palmer likes to grip the club tightly, but you are not Arnold Palmer.

The Waggle

I THINK THE MAIN value of the waggle is that it turns on your juice and gets your adrenaline flowing.

The waggle is also a small practice swing and a way to ease tension, unless you get so involved in waggling you forget your purpose.

One of my club players took 21 waggles before he could swing the club. People in his foursome would look the other way when it was his turn to hit.

Ben Hogan has a solid piece of advice: don't groove your waggle. Just get the feel and swing. Bobby Jones said if you saw him waggle more than twice, he probably hit a bad shot.

I don't like to see a player waggle up and down. To me it looks amateurish.

The great Horton Smith used no waggle at all.

Holding the Club

THERE IS AN artfulness to holding the club that goes beyond the craft of gripping it. I was teaching at a seminar in New York and, as usual, holding a club. Not that I thought I was Bob Hope, but I always found it much easier to talk to people, especially large groups, if I had a golf club in my hands.

I heard one of the pros say, "Look at Harvey. He holds that club like it's a fine musical instrument."

That's how a golf club feels to me: like a fine musical instrument.

At another seminar in Houston, Jackson Bradley, Jimmy Demaret, Jack Burke, Jr., and I were teaching, and I pointed out how beautifully Jackie Burke held the club. His hands looked perfectly natural.

"Let me add," Jackson Bradley said, "that Jackie's hands look perfect, but so do his clothes." Jackson showed us his own hands. "My fingers are a little crooked. My grip may be just as good as Jackie's, but my hands will never look as good on a club as his do."

Look at the club in the hands of Ben Crenshaw. His hands and fingers fit so gracefully, so naturally, that I am moved to regard his grip as a piece of art.

The same can be said for Mickey Wright and Dave Marr, among others.

Tommy Kite and Jack Nicklaus have a good grip on the club, but they will never look as artful because their fingers are short and they use the interlocking grip which is not as appealing to my eyes.

The Easiest Lesson

THE EASIEST GOLF lesson I ever gave was to Don January.

Don had been a star player at North Texas State University and a winner on the Texas amateur circuit, a regular round of tournaments that drew so many championship-quality golfers that I could fill up a whole book with their names.

Now Don was wondering if he could make it on the professional tour. He came to see me and asked if I would take a look at his swing and tell him my honest opinion of his game and help correct any flaws.

I watched Don hit a few putts. We went to the practice range. I asked him to hit a half-dozen short irons for me. Then I asked him to hit a half-dozen middle irons, followed by several long irons.

I could tell he was waiting for me to say something.

Instead I asked him to hit a few drives.

When he had done so, he turned and said, "Well? What do I need?"

I said, "Don, you need to pack your clubs and go to California and join the tour."

End of lesson.

Palm Reading

People are always asking me to look at the calluses on their palms, as if the location and thickness of the calluses will tell me whether their grip is correct.

I remember someone asking to see the calluses on Sam Snead's palms. Sam said, "I don't have any calluses." Sam said he holds the club as if it is a live bird in his hands, with just enough pressure that the bird can't fly away but not so tightly that the bird can't breathe. Grip the club this way and you won't have calluses, either.

Hold onto the club firmly but not tightly, with your elbows and shoulders slightly relaxed. This is especially important for women. It helps them to hit with more snap.

Where the calluses come from is a player putting his hands on the club and then twisting them into what looks like a good grip when in fact it is not a good grip.

Place your hands on the club correctly and leave them alone. There's no need to screw them around in a vain effort to make your V's point where you think they should point.

If you insist on moving your hands and fingers after taking your grip, you accomplish two things that you do not want: You camouflage a poor grip; and you get calluses.

Starting Young

THE BEST AGE to start a child in golf is the time he or she becomes interested in the game.

I don't believe in parents forcing the game on kids who would rather be doing something else. But if a little child four or five years old is eager to go out and play with Dad or Mom, then it's time to start.

Don't be too exacting on the grip or anything else. Just let the kids use their natural ability. Hands together.

Be sure the club you give them has plenty of loft. Problems start when the child uses too little loft and tries to scoop the ball up into the air. The more the child tries to help the ball up, the less it'll get up.

Also be sure the club is light enough. A small child will learn a bad grip by trying to swing a club that is too heavy. My cousin, Dr. D. A. Penick, a professor of Greek who rode around town on a bicycle and was the tennis coach at the University of Texas for fifty years, discouraged toddlers from swinging a tennis racquet for that same reason.

When you take your youngster to see a teaching pro, say that you're going to get some "help." The word "lessons" sounds too much like going to school, which is not always fun. Golf should be fun. With a child I never say "teach" or "lessons."

Group instruction for kids is all right, but in some cases the teaching can be overcomplicated to the point where it interferes with the child's natural ability. Beware especially the group instructor who is a poor player and teaches the kids what he has just read in the latest how-to-hit-it book, which the instructor may not even understand.

If you see an instructor trying to teach a whole group of kids to imitate the stance and swing of Ben Hogan, for example, take your child out of that group. The way Hogan does it is special to Hogan. Your child is special in his or her own way.

A professional should look at the child's swing maybe once a month, just to steer the game on the right track. No more.

Practicing is an individual matter. When they were kids, Ben Crenshaw was always playing more than he practiced, and Tom Kite was always practicing at least as much as he played. Hogan was a practicer. Byron Nelson was a player and also a practicer.

Whatever the child wants to do—play or practice— that's what he or she should do.

Worst of all is when I see Dad, on the range or the course, constantly nagging the child to keep his head down, keep his left arm straight, stare at the ball—bad information, all of it. This may be fun for Dad, but it is hurting the child's development.

If you are fortunate enough to be able to give your child plenty of free time to spend at a golf course, and the right amount of help from a professional teacher, your child will be beating you sooner than you may think.

Hole Them All

Two proud parents came to me at the club and announced that their young son had just scored his first birdie.

I agreed that was a wonderful event and asked them how long was the putt Junior made for the birdie.

The parents said the putt was only two feet long, so they gave Junior a "gimme" to assure his first birdie.

"I've got bad news for you," I said. "Junior still hasn't made his first birdie."

Not only did Junior not sink the birdie putt, it was now planted in his mind that he could pick up his ball two feet from the hole and pronounce the putt as made, not having to face the moment of truth.

When Junior reaches a higher level of play, where there are no "gimmes," he may develop an anxiety about short putts that will bother him the rest of his life.

My rule is that a youngster, no matter how small, should be required to hole every putt.

If Junior grows up knowing he has to make all the short ones, that will automatically become part of his game. When he plays on higher levels and faces a two-footer to win an important match, he'll be ready.

Learning Around the Cup

GOLF SHOULD BE learned starting at the cup and progressing back toward the tee.

I'm talking about with children. The same thing applies to adult beginners, but adults think that is too simple. An adult beginner—especially a man—thinks he's not getting his money's worth if you ask him to spend an hour sinking short putts. He wants to pull out his driver and smack it, which is the very last thing he will learn if he comes to me.

If a beginner tries to learn the game at the tee and move on toward the green, postponing the short game until last, this is one beginner who will be lucky ever to beat anybody.

What I like to see is a youngster learning the game on the practice green with one chipping club, a putter, and one golf ball.

A chipping stroke is just a short version of a full swing.

A child will learn a good chipping stroke and the unteachable qualities of touch and feel if the grownups will let it happen.

The best stroke in the world is not much good without touch or feel. An individual-looking stroke that the child has confidence in and a feel for how to use, and that puts the ball close to the hole, is the best stroke in the world for that child.

I will take a chipper and putter who has touch any time over someone who has a beautiful stroke but no sense of feel for where the ball is going to roll.

Many of the best putters and chippers in history learned in the caddie yard.

I like for a child to use one ball, chip it at the hole and then go put it in. This is how the child learns to score.

For a child to chip a dozen or more balls at the same hole, one after the other, is a poor method. It gives too much room for mistakes. If a child can hit a bad chip and then just drag over another ball and hit it again, it does not teach the reality of playing golf, which is that you have to pay for your mistakes.

The best thing is for the child to play games with other children on and around the practice green. I like for them to play each other for something, whether it's matchsticks or a soda pop or an imaginary U.S. Open championship—just as long as there is something at stake that makes the child concentrate on getting his or her ball into the cup in fewer strokes than the other kids. Some children are natural competitors at golf, some must learn to be, and some couldn't care less. Playing games sharpens or teaches competition. Those who don't care will drift into something else that they do care about.

I remember when Ben Crenshaw was six years old, two years before he took his first lesson from me, he and his daddy Charlie and the great tennis player Wilmer Allison, who succeeded my cousin as tennis coach at Texas, would go around and around and around the putting green, hour after hour. Ben was developing the touch and stroke that made him one of the finest putters in history. It wasn't long before he was winning quarters from the grownups.

Not everyone agrees with me on learning the game from the cup backward, of course.

Arnold Palmer's daddy taught him to hit the ball hard at a very young age. There was a shot at their golf course that called for a long carry over water. Young Arnold would stand there and bet the grownups coming through a dime or a quarter that he could hit it over the water—and he could. At the same time, Arnold became a top putter.

That's the thing about golf. Outside of the USGA rule book, there are no indisputable ways the game must be learned or played.

But if your child will learn to play on and around the green first of all, I am convinced that in most cases progress will be more rapid and the skills will be longer-lasting.

Do You Need Help?

If you play poorly one day, forget it.

If you play poorly the next time out, review your fundamentals of grip, stance, aim and ball position. Most mistakes are made before the club is swung.

If you play poorly for a third time in a row, go see your professional.

The Right Elbow

WHEN I SAY bring your right arm back to your side, I mean on the downswing—not the backswing.

Students come to me with all sorts of weird ideas they have been taught. They try to swing with a towel under their right armpit. Their right elbow is practically strapped to their body.

The result is a swing that is too short and flat.

Let your right elbow go back freely, but return it to your side when you start back to the ball.

Students tell me this towel-under-the-right-armpit drill is an old teaching. But the old Scots didn't teach it that way. Look at a photograph of Harry Vardon.

We had a good Texas amateur, Jack Munger, who played with his right elbow against his side and won a lot of trophies. Because it worked for Jack doesn't mean it is good for you.

Take Dead Aim

WHEN MY STUDENT Betsy Rawls was in a playoff for the U.S. Women's Open championship, I sent her a one-sentence telegram.

It said: "Take dead aim!"

Betsy won the playoff.

For golfers who might not understand Texas talk, let me put the advice in the telegram a different way: Once you address the golf ball, hitting it has got to be the most important thing in your life at that moment. Shut out all thoughts other than picking out a target and taking dead aim at it.

This is a good way to calm a case of nerves.

Everybody gets nervous on the first tee, whether it's Betsy Rawls in a playoff for the Open or a high handicapper teeing off at the club in a $2 Nassau with pals.

Instead of worrying about making a fool of yourself in front of a crowd of 4 or 40,000, forget about how your swing may look and concentrate instead on where you want the ball to go. Pretty is as pretty does.

I would approach my college players before a match and tell them the same thing: Take dead aim.

This is a wonderful thought to keep in mind all the way around the course, not just on the first tee. Take dead aim at a spot on the fairway or the green, refuse to allow any negative thought to enter your head, and swing away.

A high handicapper will be surprised at how often the mind will make the muscles hit the ball to the target, even with a far less than perfect swing.

The expert player won't be surprised. The expert expects to hit the target. The only surprise here is that the expert sometimes allows disorganized thinking to make him or her become distracted from the primary object of the shot, which is to hit the target.

I can't say it too many times. It's the most important advice in this book.

Take dead aim.

Make it a point to do it every time on every shot. Don't just do it from time to time, when you happen to remember.

Take dead aim.

Beware

ONE OF MY University of Texas golfers was playing in a tournament in North Carolina. He won his first match handily.

He phoned me and said, "The guy I play tomorrow I can beat easily. He has a bad grip and also a bad swing."

My boy lost the next match.

"The lesson to be learned," I told my golfer later, "is don't be afraid of the player with a good grip and a bad swing. Don't be afraid of a player with a bad grip and a good swing. The player to beware of is the one with the bad grip and the bad swing. If he's reached your level, he has grooved his faults and knows how to score."

How to Knock Five Strokes Off Your Game

THE AVERAGE GOLFER does not improve stroke by stroke.

Improvement comes in plateaus.

A player who shoots 95 does not through lessons and practice see his or her score drop slowly to 94, then 93, then 92, 91, 90. Nor does the 87-shooter come down gradually to 86, 85, 84.

Instead the 95 suddenly falls to 90. The 87 will seemingly overnight become an 81.

By the same token, a player who regularly shoots 80 can quickly fall into the middle 70's. Once you reach 75 or so, you are no longer an average golfer but are approaching the expert level, where improvement comes more slowly.

But even some 75-shooters can reach a mini-plateau and see their scores go down by three shots or so after a week of practice.

There can be many reasons why the 95 becomes a 90. Maybe the player learns to cure his slice. The 87 may become an 81 because the player learns to hit the ball 20 yards farther off the tee and now can reach more greens in regulation.

As a general rule, however, the 75-shooter can become a 72-shooter only if he improves his short game—unless it was his short-game wizardry that made him shoot 75 in the first place.

The short game. Those are the magic words.

The higher your score, the faster you can lower it—with the short game.

There's no mystery to it. Anybody who plays much golf knows that about half of his shots are struck within 60 yards of the flagstick.

And yet when I see an average golfer practicing, where is he? Most likely he is on the range, banging away with his driver.

If I ask an average golfer what percentage of his practice time he spends on his short game in comparison to hitting the longer shots, he'll probably tell me he gives the short game 10 or 20 percent. This is usually a fib. The average golfer will devote 15 minutes to stroking a few putts if he has time before he heads for the first tee, and that's about it for the short-game practice.

Well, if you want to see a radical improvement in your game and cut off five strokes in a week or two, you must make a radical change in the way you practice.

For two weeks devote 90 percent of your practice time to chipping and putting, and only 10 percent to the full swing.

If you do this, your 95 will turn into 90. I guarantee it.

I can see the average player nodding his head and saying yeah, yeah. I know that's what I ought to do.

But I don't see him doing it.

Instead I see him on the range, swinging from the heels, hitting 40 drives in a row for the thrill of those 4 or 5 that might be well struck.

I would never let my college players or the touring

pros who come to me for help hit 40 driver shots in a row. This causes fatigue and very bad habits.

My college players and touring pros, being experts, understand the immense importance of the short game. Tom Kite, for example, puts in many hours on his full swing, but he practices his wedges and his chipping and putting even more because he knows that's what causes good scores, and without good scores he wouldn't be the all-time leading money winner in golf.

So if you want to knock five shots off your game in a hurry, leave your long clubs in your bag and head for the green.

Bobby Jones said the secret of shooting low scores is the ability to turn three shots into two.

It reminds me of a college match I saw. I had a good player named Billy Munn, who was matched against R. H. Sikes of Arkansas at the old Austin Country Club.

Billy hit every fairway and 17 greens and shot 67. Sikes hit few fairways and maybe 5 greens. But Sikes shot 66 and beat Billy 1-up.

After the match I found Billy and said, "I'm very proud of you. You played a wonderful round of golf. But, Billy, don't ever think what you saw out there today was luck."

Sikes had a great short game, as he went on to prove on the professional tour.

You may never develop a short game to equal Sikes's, but if you practice hard on chipping and putting you can bring your score down fast. It's all up to you.

Emerson said, "Thinking is the hardest work in the world. That's why so few of us do it."

Too many golfers think chipping and putting is hard work. That's why so few of them do it.

Reassurance

ONE OF MY favorite students, Sandra Palmer, a very successful player on the LPGA Tour, phoned me one night from the site of the U.S. Women's Open.

Sandra was worried about the speed of the greens. She said they were the slickest, fastest greens she had ever seen. The tournament started the next morning, and Sandra was getting the jitters wondering if she could putt greens like this. Should she try to change her stroke?

I knew Sandra was a fine putter, and what she needed was reassurance.

"Well, Sandra," I said, "if the greens are that fast, you probably should hit your putts a little easier."

That's all it took.

Students are always asking if they should switch to heavier putters when they go play at a club with faster greens. It's probably true that if you went through the members' bags at Oakmont—famous for its fast greens—you would find heavy putters in most of them. But you should stick with your favorite putter when you go to a course with faster (or slower) greens. It's easier to get the feel for different greens than for a different putter.

The Practice Swing

How many times have you seen an average golfer take two or three beautiful practice swings and then step up to the ball and make a swing that is totally different and causes an ugly shot?

It happens over and over.

As a caddie, a pro, a teacher and starter at the first tee over the past seventy-five years, I have probably seen more golf swings than any person alive. The practice swing and real swing I just described, I must have seen a million times.

And what does the average golfer say? "If I could just hit the ball with my practice swing, I'd be a terrific player."

The reason he doesn't hit the ball with his practice swing is simple: With his practice swing he doesn't have to square his clubface on impact. He allows himself to swing freely. When there's a golf ball in front of him, he knows—at least subconsciously—that he must square that clubface, and tension sets in, causing all sorts of faults.

Now let me ask another question: How many times have you seen a player make two or three beautiful practice swings that don't touch anything but air?

These swings are useful for loosening up, but they are no good when it comes to hitting the ball.

From now on when you take a practice swing, make it

a point to aim at something. Cut off a dandelion or a blade of grass, or if you are in your living room aim at a spot on the rug (but please don't take a divot and tell your wife Harvey made you do it).

Aiming at something with your practice swing will help you learn to square the clubface. Never take another practice swing without aiming it at something.

One more thing about practice swings.

Taking two or three practice swings before every shot when you are on the course playing golf takes up too much time. In these days of the four- or five-hour round, we need to speed up the game, not slow it down.

At many courses in Scotland and England there is a sign on the first tee that says, "A round of golf requires no more than 3 hours, 15 minutes. If you are on the course longer than this, a marshal will come escort you off."

You don't see those Scots loitering in the fairway to take practice swings.

The Average Golfer

I USE THE term "average golfer" a lot, but sometimes I wonder, what is an average golfer?

I read somewhere that statistics show the average male golfer shoots about 92.

I don't believe it. Not if he counts every stroke and plays by USGA rules. Playing our Pete Dye course from the men's tees and holing every shot, the average golfer won't break 100.

A party of four Japanese gentlemen once showed up as special guests to play our course, which they had heard about in Tokyo.

I asked how well they played so I would know which of our four sets of tees—women's, seniors', men's or championship—I would suggest.

They said they were average players and would use the championship tees because they wanted to see the whole course.

Well, I knew they wouldn't see the whole course from the back tees, because they couldn't hit the ball over our canyons from back there. But they were guests.

It took them twenty minutes and three lost balls to get past our first hole, which is relatively easy—a sharp dogleg left uphill over a ravine. About six hours later, I realized our Japanese gentlemen were still on the course, and I went to find them.

They were on the 14th hole. One was off in the trees,

another was down in a canyon, the third was searching in the deep rough on a hillside, and the fourth greeted me with a smile.

"Very good course," he said.

"How are you doing?" I asked.

"Very good," he said.

Dick Metz said a club pro is half-mule and half-slave. Instead of escorting them off the course, I politely urged them to try to finish before dark, and then I went back to the clubhouse.

Later I heard them figuring up their scores. Every one of them shot in the low 90's.

The fact is, by USGA rules not a one of them broke 100—on the first nine.

But of course they weren't really average golfers, either.

How to Tell Where You're Aimed

TAKE YOUR STANCE and hold a clubshaft along the front of your *thighs*. Look where the club is pointing, and you will see where you are aimed.

Laying a club on the ground at your feet will tell you very little.

Much is made of how to aim.

Hit the ball solidly, and I can show you where you were aimed. Once you learn this, your mind will tell you how to aim.

Seasoned Citizens

ONE OF THE many wonderful things about golf is that it is a game you can play for the rest of your life.

In fact, Seasoned Citizens—a term I much prefer to "Senior"—may get even more enjoyment out of the game than they did when they were young, because the deeper you get into golf, the more you learn to value the freedom, the companionship, the joy of being outdoors in beautiful surroundings, and the profound mysteries of the game itself.

Like chess, golf is a game that is forever challenging but can never be conquered.

As a golfer grows older and becomes a Seasoned Citizen, age does take its toll on the eyesight, the muscles, the flexibility and all too often on the waistline.

But there are many ways a Seasoned Citizen can continue to score as well as when young, or perhaps score better due to the wisdom of age and the new equipment that is available.

First and foremost, a Seasoned Citizen must make every effort to maintain good physical condition.

If you can walk the golf course, do it. Get out of that golf cart. If your companions in your regular foursome insist on riding, it's all right to go along with them, but you should hop out of the cart and walk at every opportunity.

Carry two or three clubs in hand that you know you

may need, and don't be afraid of slowing your companions down. The truth is that a briskly walking foursome will usually go around the course faster than a foursome in golf carts.

Golfers in carts are always driving here and there from one ball to the other, taking up a lot of time. If a rule is in effect that the cart is not allowed to leave the path, golfers are inclined to dawdle over club selection and make unnecessary trips back and forth from the ball to the bag.

Carts are very valuable tools for Seasoned Citizens who can't physically go around the course without them. One of our members is hooked up to an oxygen tank, but the golf cart allows him to continue to enjoy playing the game.

I've noticed that walkers tend to band together. If you walk and either carry a lightweight bag or pull your clubs on a trolley, you'll soon find a regular game with like-minded players.

Walking keeps a Seasoned Citizen's legs strong, and strong legs make for a more powerful swing.

I will stress here—and this is vital—that a Seasoned Citizen must let the left heel come off the ground in the backswing.

Let the left heel come up and the left arm bend for a longer, freer swing.

Some modern teachers demand that their students keep the left heel on the ground. I don't agree with that teaching for players of any age, but especially not for a Seasoned Citizen.

One of the most important factors in an older golfer's swing is the body turn. The older one gets, the harder it is to turn. Keeping the left heel down makes it all the harder. Don't raise the heel, just let it come up as it will want to do.

A straight left arm inhibits the turn. If a Seasoned Citizen has become heavy in the chest and stomach, there should be no effort made to keep a straight left arm at the top of the backswing. A player should try to swing longer, not shorter, as the years go by.

Another block to the swing is keeping the head down too long. I doubt I tell one student a month to keep his head down, and I almost never say it to an older player. Keeping the head down prevents a good follow-through because the golfer can't swing past hip-high with the head still down and not give up something good in the finish to do it.

Other than strong legs and plenty of stretching exercises, the first consideration for the older golfer is selecting the proper clubs.

You don't want to fiddle too much with a swing that has been useful to you for decades, but now is the time to add a 5- or 6-wood and especially a 7-wood to your bag. Seasoned Citizens get their loft from their clubs, not from their swing. Adding loft is a reliable substitute for youth and strength.

The older golfer must play with softer shafts. If you used "S" shafts when you were younger, switch to the "R" shafts. If you had been using "R" shafts, you may need to change to "A" shafts. You are not hitting as hard as when you were young, and you can't get the most out of the stiffer shafts.

Men should use D-O or lower swingweights. Women should use no more than C-6 or C-8.

Many Seasoned Citizens have problems with arthritis in their hands. Built-up grips are available to help you hold the club. Composition grips are best for arthritic golfers because they give a bit. Leather is not resilient enough.

I don't like to see the Seasoned player change to longer shafts in an effort to get more distance. A longer club causes a big change in the swing plane, from upright to flat. Flat swings require more turn, which is difficult for an older player.

If you can hit the ball solidly, you can get enough distance.

The Seasoned Citizen may want to try the ten-finger grip, which allows the hands to move faster.

One disadvantage older players may have is that they learned the game before the tremendous improvement in golf course maintenance, when it was necessary to hit down on the ball because the grass was sparse. Today's heavy, well-watered fairways make hitting down on the ball an out-of-date technique.

Many older golfers learned to play the ball far back in their stance for an iron shot. Modern fairways have done away with the need for that technique, also. Years ago we would play the ball off the right foot so we could hit down on it on the bare lies. Today the iron shots should be played no farther back than center.

A Seasoned Citizen should at regular intervals visit a professional who understands the problems of older golfers. You don't want a teacher who tries to rebuild a golf swing that you have been using for decades. You want a teacher who will help you get the best out of the swing you already have.

Perhaps most important of all, a Seasoned Citizen should devote at least 75 percent of practice time to the short game.

I harp on the significance of the short game to golfers of all ages. But this is an area where an older player who may have never broken 90 can expect to cut strokes. A retired person has the time to practice the short game. Short shots don't require strength or flexibility.

Don't plead that you are so old and your nerves so frayed that you can't putt. Every golf course has a few old geezers who can chip and putt the eyes out of the cup.

Certainly the older golfer can't hit the ball as far as the young, flat-bellied player. But once you reach the fringe of the green, you and the younger player become no worse than equals. And you can even have the advantage if you are faithful in practicing your short game.

Just as I suggest for children, the Seasoned Citizen will get the most out of chipping and putting practice by using just one golf ball to practice with instead of a whole basketful at a time.

Pitch or chip that one ball to the cup, and then go putt it until you make it, just as you would have to do if you were on the course playing a match. This sharpens your focus and improves your touch.

You have plenty of time. Make a game out of practice. You may be a Seasoned Citizen, but you know you're still a child at heart.

The Left Heel

THE LEFT HEEL is the subject of distinctly different schools of teaching.

Many modern teachers want their students to keep their left heel on the ground throughout the swing.

The old-school teachers like Percy Boomer and the great Scottish pros want the left heel to come up in the backswing and return to the ground at the start of the downswing.

I am of the old school, not because it produces a more classic swing—which it does—but because letting the left heel come up is the best way to get the job done.

The important thing is that you do not consciously lift the left heel. You keep the left heel on the ground, but you let it naturally come up as you make your back turn.

I think the reason Jack Nicklaus has such good control at the top is that he lets that left heel come up, releasing a full turn. He doesn't have to complete his backswing by letting loose of the club.

Ben Hogan never worried about his left heel. It either came up or it didn't, depending on the swing he was making.

Shelley Mayfield made the left-heel-on-the-ground swing popular in the middle 50s when he was a winner on the tour. Shelley, who became the head pro at Brook Hollow in Dallas, told me he didn't keep his left heel on the ground on purpose. It was just his natural, individual style.

Often when people imitate the swing of a top player, they will pick out a peculiarity to copy. The so-called flying elbow of Nicklaus or the open stance of Lee Trevino will be what they imitate.

Shelley told me he wished his left heel had let itself come up in his backswing, but it just wouldn't do it.

In my opinion, keeping the left heel flat on the ground throughout the swing will shorten the player's period of success.

Backspin

An average golfer was pestering Tommy Armour to teach him how to put backspin on his iron shots.

The obvious answer is that if you hit the ball solidly, the loft on the club will put backspin on it. But this was too simple. The average golfer was sure Tommy must know some secret that made a good middle-iron shot land on the green and dance backward.

Finally Tommy said, "Let me ask you something. When you hit an approach shot from 140 yards or so, are you usually past the pin, or are you usually short of it?"

"I'm nearly always short of the pin," the average golfer replied.

"Then what do you need with backspin?" Tommy said.

Heavy Clubs

EVERY GOLFER from the young adult through Seasoned Citizens, should own a heavy practice club that weighs at least 22 ounces.

It hardly need be said that a heavy club is no good for children.

Swinging a weighted club, with your regular grip and stance, is the best exercise I know to build the golf muscles. Squeezing a tennis ball and similar exercises might be all right, but I'd be afraid the wrong muscles might get developed.

In golf you don't need muscles that lift weights. You want muscles that can pop a whip—or play golf.

Swing the weighted club the night before a round, not in the morning before you tee off. Save your strength for the golf course.

Don't swing it so hard you'll hurt yourself. If it is inconvenient to go outside, swing the weighted club indoors—in slow motion.

A slow-motion swing develops the golf muscles, implants the correct club positions in your golfing brain—and doesn't smash the chandelier.

Every time you swing that weighted club, slow or moderately fast, aim the clubhead at a fixed spot. Learn a good habit while you are building golf muscles.

Hints on Greenskeeping

DR. ALISTER MACKENZIE, the renowned Scottish golf architect who designed Augusta National and Cypress Point in this country, many years ago wrote a short piece called "Hints on Greenskeeping," which I kept on the wall of our golf shop.

What he says is timeless advice, and I quote it here:

> The amount of harm done by rabbits is infinitesimal compared with the good they do. They keep land sour and create the best golfing turf, with freedom from weeds and worms.
>
> Remember that golf is a game and no player ever gets any fun in searching for lost balls.
>
> Cut the fairways and greens in the irregular curves of nature, and not in straight lines.
>
> Don't remove the grass cuttings. They encourage a thick carpet of turf. Roots then become thick and strong and the leaf growth fine and plentiful. [*This advice has changed since MacKenzie's day, because doing this encourages disease on the greens.*]
>
> The cost of the best advice is infinitesimal compared with the amount of money frequently wasted without it.
>
> Never take the advice of a gardener or agricul-

tural expert unless he has made a study of the special requirements of golf.

Agricultural grasses want an alkaline soil, whereas golfing grasses require an acid soil.

Lime, basic slag, bone meal and other alkaline fertilizers create rich agricultural grasses, daisies, plantains and worms.

The most common cause of bad greens and muddy fairways is worms. These must be eradicated.

Beware of overfeeding. The most suitable vegetation for golf is to be found on poor, sour, sandy or heathland soils.

Never follow the advice of a golfer, however good a player he may be, unless he is broadminded enough to recognize that not only has the beginner to be considered, but also a very high standard of golf architecture improves everyone's play.

Golf course construction is a difficult art (like sculpture). Endeavor to make every feature indistinguishable from a natural one.

Most courses have too many bunkers. They should be constructed from a strategical and not from a penal point of view.

Fiercely criticized holes often improve the standard of play and ultimately become the most popular.

Never destroy undulations, hazards or other features because at first sight they appear to be unfair. Their destruction may detract appreciably from the strategy, interest and excitement of the game.

Never alter a hole unless you are convinced that the change will increase the joy and the thrills of overcoming difficulties.

The best golf courses are those the holes of which have been designed and constructed to conform to the character of the ground at one's disposal.

To attempt to copy a famous hole where conditions are dissimilar is usually fatal.

The Wrist Cock

I PREFER A swing with a full, early wrist cock, but I don't like to use the words "wrist cock" because so many students become so entranced with getting their wrists cocked that they forget the rest of the swing.

One way to mess up students is to tell them to cock their wrists.

Women, especially, try to cock their wrists at the top of their backswing—and thus they overswing and lose snap.

When you swing back to waist high—the shaft parallel to the ground—the toe of the club must be pointed straight up to the sky.

If it is, your wrists will be cocked and you don't need to think about it. Go ahead and make your turn.

To get a clear picture in mind of how the wrists cock, double your left hand into a fist. This is an automatic wrist cock.

Make a golf swing with your left fist and you can immediately see what position the club is in when your wrists cock, then uncock, and cock again at the finish.

Look at your fist in a full-length mirror. The "wrist cock" will cease to be a source of confusion.

Hit a Full Approach

The average golfer seldom hits a middle-iron approach shot past the pin.

Some teachers recommend that the average golfer use one club stronger for his approach.

In other words, some say if you are 140 yards out and think the shot calls for a 7-iron, choose a 6-iron instead and hit it easier.

I don't care for this idea. I would much rather you take the 7-iron and hit it harder, with the thought in mind that you are going to get the ball all the way to the hole.

When you take a stronger club and try to hit it easy, your muscles will involuntarily tell you that you are using the wrong club, and you are likely to flinch and pull up on the shot.

If you want to hit the stronger club anyway, grip down an inch on the handle—and go ahead and hit it hard.

I like to see a golfer hit the ball hard if he doesn't swing so fiercely he loses his tempo and balance.

When Jimmy Thompson was the longest hitter on the tour, he enjoyed visiting me for guidance because he knew I was one teacher who would never tell him not to hit it so hard.

But always play within yourself.

The main reason so many approach shots come up short is that four out of five are hit off-center.

Easy Bunkers

WHILE BUNKER PLAY continues to scare the wits out of most average golfers, in my opinion it has become much too easy for the touring professional.

Touring pros will aim at greenside bunkers because they have such skill at hitting a sand wedge close to the cup. Even so, the touring pros are constantly complaining about the quality of the sand in the bunkers. They want it just the right texture to make splashing the ball out of a bunker even easier.

Except for unusually deep bunkers or for bad lies, the touring pro would rather hit a simple (for him) bunker shot than try to pitch the ball to the pin out of the high grass around most greens.

This is not the original intention of placing bunkers beside the greens. A bunker was an obstacle to be avoided.

A Houston Country Club member, Edwin MacClain, invented and patented the first sand wedge in 1928. Bobby Jones used a MacClain sand wedge in the British Open in 1930. Horton Smith carried one on tour.

In 1931 MacClain's sand wedge was ruled illegal because its face was concave, like a soup spoon. Photographs showed the golfer hitting the ball twice with this wedge—once on bottom and once on top.

Gene Sarazen invented his sand wedge in 1932, and it was immediately a success.

Even after the sand wedge came along, bunkers were

still no picnic because they might contain as much dirt as sand. But then the sand bunkers became consistent, and the pros lost all fear of them.

These days there is the growing feeling that the high-tech equipment, the juiced-up ball and the powerful swings of the touring pros are making many of our finest old golf courses obsolete.

I have a suggestion that would put the teeth back into our old courses and make greenside bunkers once again places for the touring pros to beware:

Stop raking the sand smooth.

Either don't rake the sand at all, or, better, rake the sand in furrows.

No more would I hear my old Texas friend, former PGA champion Dave Marr, say on television, "Freddie made a good play there, choosing to hit his shot into the bunker instead of chancing to land it on the slick green where it might roll into the collar of rough grass."

Instead I would hear Dave say, "Aw, oh, Freddie hit it into the bunker. He'll be awfully happy if he can get down in two from those furrows."

This will never happen, of course. Touring pros and club members wouldn't stand for it. But it would make our old courses instantly more difficult by punishing a shot that doesn't settle onto the green.

They don't rake most bunkers along the fairways at Pine Valley, which I suppose is the best golf course in the world, but they do make them smooth around the greens.

Pine Valley is plenty hard enough for the amateurs who play there, even with smooth bunkers.

But they never have a professional tournament. Touring pros with their talent at sand play might embarrass even such an icon as Pine Valley.

Bunker Play

PRACTICE YOUR BUNKER game to become more aggressive with it. You don't have to look at it as being in anticipation of your misses.

If you practice it and learn a few fundamentals, playing a ball out of a greenside bunker is not a difficult shot, even for the average golfer.

First, grip your sand wedge high on the handle as you would for a normal iron shot. This encourages you to take a full swing all the way to a high follow-through without quitting on the shot when the club strikes the sand.

Grip it tightly with the little finger and ring finger of your left hand so the club won't roll over and close in the sand.

Play the ball with the shaft pointing at your zipper and your hands slightly ahead. Take a square stance and open your clubface so that it points right of the target.

Then open your stance by moving your left foot back and taking your hips and shoulders with it, so that now your body is aimed left of the target but the clubface has come around to aim straight at it.

Shift a little more weight onto the left foot than on the right.

Now make a basically normal swing along the line established by your shoulders and body. Hit three or four inches behind the ball and clip the sand out from beneath it. The ball will come out and land on the green in a spray of sand.

Practice this shot for a few hours and you will see what I mean about becoming aggressive with it.

You won't need to worry again about merely escaping from the bunker somehow. You will be shooting at the pin.

The longer the shot, the less you hit behind the ball. The shorter the shot, the more sand you must take.

Don't Relax

You hear it all the time on the range and on the course—relax, relax, relax.

I have even heard a golfer attempt to help a companion by saying, "Try real hard to relax."

If you try real hard to relax, you will become either very tense or else so limp you might fall over on the grass and go to drowsing.

Neither of those states is conducive to hitting a golf shot.

You do want to keep tension from creeping into your muscles, of course, and from allowing fear in your heart.

But I prefer to put it this way:

Be at ease.

If you feel at ease, you are relaxed—but ready.

The secret is the feeling of "controlled violence," as Jackie Burke, Jr., says.

Positive Thinking

WHEN I AM teaching, I never say never and I don't say don't, if I can help it.

I use the words "never" and "don't" in this book rather often, but that is because the reader has the leisure to reflect upon the point I am trying to get across.

But I would never say never and I don't say don't to a student on the range with club in hand and a need to learn while under the stress of being watched and mentally graded.

I try to put everything in positive, constructive terms. I go into this subject more deeply in my remarks on teaching, but the point I am trying to get across to the reader here is that when you are hitting a golf shot, a negative thought is pure poison.

I could have called this discussion "No Negative Thoughts"—but even that can be construed as a negative thought in the mind of a golfer.

Jack Burke, Sr., said it this way: "Give yourself the benefit of the doubt."

But even that statement has the dangerous word "doubt" in it.

I want you to believe with all your heart that the shot you are about to hit will be a good one. I want you to have total confidence.

This may sound ridiculous to the player who doesn't break 100. The difference is between confidence and optimism. Confidence is when you have hit this particular shot many times in the past with success, and you know you are capable of doing it again. Any 85-shooter has hit every shot in the bag with success many times. The ability is there. Optimism would be if you had never hit this shot successfully in your life, and are hoping this will be the first time.

The 100-shooter can be helped enormously by positive thinking, but he or she needs some groundwork of teaching upon which to base these positive thoughts before they can be distinguished as the feeling of confidence.

Indecision is a killer.

For example, when you pull that 5-iron out of the bag and register the target in your mind and address the ball, you must totally believe this is the right club for the shot. Put your best swing on it.

If it turns out the 5-iron was a club too much or too little but you hit it solidly, you won't be more than 10 yards off.

However, if you can't make up your mind whether the shot calls for a 4-, a 5- or a 6-iron, and you choose the 5 as a compromise, and then are still unsure when you take your stance, you might as well go sit down.

Many conflicting voices are chattering inside the mind of the average golfer. He or she is thinking of the latest swing "tips" heard on the veranda, and wondering if the club is going back too much inside and which "swing thought" might work at the moment, and probably worrying if the teenager remembered to put gas in the auto.

The golfer must learn to turn off all these voices.

A golf swing happens right now, not in the past or in the future.

Think positively and as my big brother Tom, the pro at Austin Muny for thirty years, used to say, "Rare back and hit it."

Psychology

A SPORTSWRITER WAS in town to interview Tom Kite at Austin Country Club. Sandra Palmer and I were standing around, sort of listening to the interview. The sportswriter turned to me and said, "Harvey, I understand you are practically a psychiatrist when it comes to golf."

"I don't know about that," I said. "I'm just a grown caddie still studying golf."

"You used psychology on me this morning," Tommy said.

"When was that?" I asked.

"When I asked you to help me with my putting," Tommy said. "You asked me if I had changed anything since the last time you saw me. I said, yes, I had started choking down on my putter."

"Tommy, don't use that word," I said. "You should never use the word 'choke' in connection with your golf game. Don't think of choking down on your putter—think of gripping down on it."

"That's what you told me this morning," he said. "That's psychology, isn't it?"

It always made me uncomfortable when Jimmy Demaret talked about his "choke stroke."

What Jimmy meant was he had in his repertoire a simple, reliable type of swing that he could call upon when he was under intense pressure. This swing wouldn't do anything fancy and wouldn't hit the ball as far as normal, but it was a repeating swing that would put his ball somewhere in the fairway or on the green.

He should have called it a "no choke stroke."

But I wouldn't have liked that either, because it still had the word "choke" in it, and also the word "no."

The golfing area of the brain is a fragile thing that is terribly susceptible to suggestion. Golfers are gullible.

I tell my players to go to dinner with good putters.

We have all played with people who would try to talk you into losing. They'll stand on the tee with an innocent expression and say, "Gee, look how tight that boundary marker is on the left. I sure hope I don't hit it over there." Or they might say, "That's an interesting change you've made in your backswing, Harvey." Maybe the best one I ever heard was when someone asked, "Do you breathe in or out on your backswing?"

We call these remarks "The Needle."

The Needle seldom bothers an experienced player. Instead, it's a giveaway that the person using The Needle is feeling insecure.

Playing golf you learn a form of meditation. For the four hours you are on the course, you learn to focus on the game and clean your mind of worrisome thoughts.

Golf has probably kept more people sane than psychiatrists have.

Stay Behind the Ball

TRY TO SHOW me a champion who doesn't move his head during his golf swing. You can't do it. Sam Snead comes as close as anyone ever has, but he moves it too.

However, all these great players move their head slightly backward before and during impact—never forward.

Home-run hitters do the same thing. You'd see Hank Aaron blast one over the scoreboard, and people would say, "He really stayed behind that one."

A golfer also must stay behind the ball.

You couldn't kill a fly with a flyswatter if you lunged your head forward. To get power with a fly swatter you hold your head steady, or pull it back. Byron Nelson dropped his head back nearly a foot coming into the ball.

Before you can stay behind the ball, you must *get* behind it. I mean set up with your head behind the ball and keep your head behind the ball.

If you move your head forward during your downswing or through impact, you will hit a weak, ugly shot, probably a pulled slice.

A student told me about a round of golf he played with Lee Trevino.

On the second tee, a par three, the student hit what he thought was a pretty good shot, about 30 feet short of the pin.

Trevino tossed another ball onto the ground.

"Tee it up and hit it again—don't move your head forward this time," Trevino said.

"Lee, I've been trying all my life to stop moving my head forward," the student said. "How can I do it?"

Trevino said, "Read my lips. D-O-N'-T M-O-V-E Y-O-U-R H-E-A-D F-O-R-W-A-R-D. Every time you hit a ball today, I want you to think 'Lee is watching and saying read my lips.'"

The student was deeply impressed. He made another swing, this time without moving his head forward. With an authoritative crack, the ball took off in a slight draw, came down 10 feet past the pin and backed up.

"I have created a monster," Lee said.

The student finished the first nine one under par.

At the turn Lee put his clubs in the trunk of his car and said, "I have to leave now, Frankenstein. Don't forget what I told you."

I asked the student what happened next.

"By the fourteenth hole my head was moving forward again," he admitted. "I shot my usual forty-one on the back."

Maybe it was the word "don't" that made the suggestion not last long.

A positive way to put it is: *stay behind the ball.*

Hitting From the Top

PROBABLY THE BIGGEST fault for all players has dozens of different names around the world. In England it is called Casting, which is a good description because the movement you make with your right arm and hand is similar to casting with a fly rod.

My friend Darrell Royal, an excellent golf player as well as the head coach of National Championship football teams at the University of Texas, has a colorful name for the fault I am talking about.

Darrell calls it OTTFIG. This translates to: "Over the Top, Forget It."

For this discussion, I will refer to the fault as Hitting From the Top.

Hitting From the Top is what happens when you reach the top of your backswing, and start back down to the ball by throwing your hands at it.

Many golfers play their whole lives Hitting From the Top. Some have managed to play well despite this flaw. Amateur Bud McKinney, a Texan who wore big flashy diamond rings, rang up an impressive record while Hitting From the Top. There are players on the professional tour who get outside the ball on their downswing, which is about the same thing as Hitting From the Top.

But just because some players are athletic enough to make this move and get away with it, doesn't make it any less disastrous for the average golfer.

No one has ever found an instant cure for this particular ailment.

Hard practice on sound fundamentals is a great help, of course, but that is not the answer a one-visit student wants to hear from an instructor.

Here are a number of things that cause Hitting From the Top:

- A grip that is too weak, especially the left hand.
- Misuse of the forearms, meaning the use of the wrists instead of the forearms at the beginning of the backswing and at impact.
- Aiming to the right.
- A stiff left leg at impact. I notice that the expert players who are least likely to Hit From the Top keep their knees slightly bent as they come through the ball. Telling a student to hit against a strong left side, which used to be common theory in teaching, tends to make the student start the downswing from outside the ball, straighten the left leg and throw the club out and over the correct swing path.

  (To demonstrate this point, make a slow-motion swing keeping your knees slightly bent until after the ball is hit. The club will stay inside. Take another slow-motion swing and straighten your left leg about halfway down. Your upper body will throw itself out and over the ball.)
- The clubface too open at address.

But the question the instructor constantly confronts is, how to persuade the student to stop Hitting From the Top without becoming too technical or offering more advice than can be absorbed in one lesson.

I know five ways that have been successful for me.

The first and simplest is to make the student try to hit the ball on the toe of the club for a while. This is often a one-aspirin remedy for the sickness.

Another simple one is to place two balls on the ground about two inches apart and have the student hit the inside ball without touching the other.

A third and still simple method is for me to hold a shaft about a foot off the ground in front of the student and have him swing beneath it.

The fourth cure, the strongest and most basic, is to make the student learn to hook the ball. Strengthen the grip, rolling both hands to the right in exaggerated fashion. Tell the student to go ahead and hook the ball clear off the practice range. I don't care if it's a pulled hook or a big wild hook, just as long as it is a hook.

I tell the student to rotate the left forearm to the right going back. Sometimes I have the student think of rotating the entire left arm. This fans the clubhead open on the backswing. Then bring the club down rotating the left arm and hand (the right hand automatically becomes involved) to the left and close the clubface hard at impact.

This process produces some of the most screaming fishhook-looking shots you ever saw.

But to hit these fishhooks, the student has to come into the ball from the inside.

Once a student learns to create hooks at will, he has usually stopped Hitting From the Top. The problem now becomes curing the hook. But this is relatively easy.

The fifth method is a slow-motion drill, and it's such an important drill that I want to hold it apart and explain it in a piece of its own.

I was demonstrating these methods at a PGA teaching

seminar, using a waitress who had never played golf before as the student.

When we came to the fourth way, I was explaining to the pros in the crowd how this can cure the slice, and the waitress stopped me.

"Mr. Penick," she cried, "I don't want to be a hooker!"

Hypnotism

AT A PGA school in California, I was trying to help a good player who had developed a slice. About forty pros were watching.

After making a small change in his grip, I said, "This man has such a good swing, he can hit the ball with his eyes closed."

I told him to make a couple of practice swings without a ball, just concentrating on clipping the tee.

Then I put a ball on the tee.

"Now shut your eyes and make that same good swing," I said.

He hit the prettiest shot you ever saw, with a little hook on the end.

"I know what you did, Harvey," one of the pros said. "You hypnotized that man."

The Slow-Motion Drill

THE SLOW-MOTION DRILL is a drill you can do at home, and it takes much patience and many repetitions, but the time you spend at it will pay off on the golf course.

Mickey Wright practiced this drill often. As an all-purpose drill that is good for whatever ails your golf swing, this is probably the best. You can do it indoors, so you can do it in bad weather or at night.

When I say slow motion, I mean *really slow, slow motion.* If you think you are doing it in slow motion, do it even slower.

Swing the club very slowly to the top of the backswing. *Always* keep your eye on the blade of grass or the pattern in the carpet that represents the golf ball; watching the clubhead go back is a terrible habit you can accidentally pick up in this drill and take to the course with you.

As you reach the top of the backswing, replace your left heel solidly on the ground and at the same time bring your right elbow in close to your body. Very, very slowly.

Bring the club down in extreme slow motion about one third of the way toward the ball. Then stop a moment and hold it and feel it.

Now start from your holding position and do it again—swing slowly to the top, plant the left heel, bring the right elbow close to the body, and stop about one third of the way toward the ball.

Do this four times in a row. Don't get impatient and speed up. Very slowly is the key.

After four repetitions, go ahead and make the full swing at last—still in very slow motion—into a high finish with the elbows out front and your head coming up slowly as if to watch a good shot. Hold the pose. Feel it.

Now do the whole thing again and again and again.

What is happening is that your golfing brain and your muscles are learning to start your downswing by planting your weight and moving your lower body to the left, and you are coming to the ball from inside with your hands quiet, trailing and still cocked, not leading and spending energy.

Your golfing brain and your muscles learn just as well from repeating the swing in slow motion as from whapping away on the range. In fact, it can be higher quality learning because no mistakes are being made in the slow-motion swing.

Powder the Ball

MANY AVERAGE GOLFERS are not sure which part of their clubface is striking the ball, whether it's with the putter, an iron shot or a driver.

It's very simple to find out.

Take a can of talcum powder with you to the range or the putting green. Powder the ball. Hit it. Look at the clubface.

You'll know immediately.

Ball Position

POSITION OF THE ball is second in importance only to the grip.

Mistakes in grip and ball position are mistakes made before the swing that may ruin any grand plans you have for the shot.

Many instructors teach that the ball should be played off the left heel for all shots.

I don't agree with this. Good players can do it nowadays off good lies. But if you play the ball off your left heel with a 9-iron, you are going to have to have a terribly fast hip shift to meet the club with the ball on the downblow.

The driver and a teed-up 3-wood are the only clubs you want to play off your left heel. This is because you want to hit the ball slightly on the upswing or at the lowest point of the swing with these clubs.

With the rest of the clubs you move back a fraction of an inch at a time until you reach dead center, which is where the 9-iron belongs.

If you have any doubt where to position the ball for any iron, take a couple of practice swings and note where the clubface brushes the ground.

Another way is to put your iron down on the grass with a square face, and you will see where the manufacturer designed the club to be played.

Swing the Bucket

To start a golf swing you need a forward press of some sort that sets off the action.

My favorite image of what I want the forward press to feel like is to imagine you are in your stance holding a bucket of water with your hands on either side of the bucket.

If you're going to swing this bucket back like a golf backswing, you just naturally won't do it from a dead stop. Your hands and hips and shoulders and legs will rock forward a tiny bit to provide the reaction that gives momentum to the backswing. This starts the turn and the shift of the weight to the right foot that you would need to swing a bucket of water.

Your hands will follow your turn into the backswing as the bucket goes up. Your left heel will rise.

If you are gripping the bucket tightly, you will turn fast. If your grip is light, your turn will be slow and free.

To bring the bucket back down, you wouldn't throw it with your hands. You would shift your weight onto your left foot and turn your left hip, and you would naturally stay behind the bucket as you swing it down and through.

You can picture the release of power as the bucket reaches the forward swing and the water flies out.

A teacher I respect, Chuck Cook, suggests further in the swing-the-bucket image that if you tell your muscles to spill water to the left at the finish, you will hit a hook or draw, and if you spill it to the right, you will hit a fade.

The swing-the-bucket image works. It is especially easy to use to start a forward press.

Remember, don't overdo it. Just take a sip of medicine, not a great gulp.

The Weed Cutter

OF ALL THE thousands of swing-training aids and gimmicks I have seen, the best is one you can buy at the hardware store if you don't already have it in your garage or toolshed.

It is the common weed cutter.

Many years ago Victor East, the genius behind Spalding clubs, sent six weed cutters to me and six to Wild Bill Mehlhorn, who was teaching at a club in Florida.

A few weeks later Mehlhorn sent his weed cutters back to Victor with a note that said, "These things are ruining my business. Students who use them don't need me anymore."

The motion you make lopping off dandelions with your weed cutter is the perfect action of swinging a golf club through the hitting area.

Furthermore, the weed cutter is heavy and builds golf muscles.

While you are swinging the weed cutter, pretend you are being paid by the hour, not by the job.

In other words, take your time.

Placing Your Feet

MOST PLAYERS, INCLUDING many experts, fail to grasp what a big difference in the length of the swing is caused by the positions of the feet.

Try this and see for yourself. Take a normal stance and turn back to the top of your backswing with your shaft pointing at the target. Look in the mirror. Now set up again. This time turn your left foot out and down the line enough to cut out a good slice of pie. Make your backswing as before. Look in the mirror again. What do you see? Your backswing is several inches shorter.

Set up again with your left foot in a natural position, but bring your right foot square to the line or even point it a bit toward the target. Make your backswing. See? Again your backswing is several inches shorter.

Many players set up with their left foot splayed way out and their right foot square or turned in—a combination guaranteed to shorten the backswing dramatically.

An average player will adopt this stance because he thinks this is what he sees the pros do. Then he will wonder, where did my turn go?

These foot positions have no real effect on where you are aiming, but they are very important in the length of your swing.

The Turn

THE TURN AWAY from the ball and back through it again is a simple movement that has been made to seem complicated by differing teaching theories and personal idiosyncrasies.

As Horton Smith would say, the turn is just like that song children used to sing, "The ankle bone connected to the knee bone, the knee bone connected to the hip bone, the hip bone connected to the back bone, the back bone connected to the shoulder bone . . . Now hear the word of the Lord."

Do it this way and keep it simple:

Stand erect with your knees slightly flexed and your eyes on the ball. Think of your swing-the-bucket image to start your forward press. Turn your body to the right with your weight shifting to your right foot, and let your left heel gently come up about an inch. It's like turning to say howdy to someone on your right. Your arms keep swinging until your shaft is behind you and points to the target.

Now let your weight shift back to your left foot at the same time your right elbow starts back toward your side, and continue turning as if to say howdy to someone on your left.

You will read and hear many complex instructions about the turn—coiling the torso and shoulders against the tension of the hips, for example—but not from me.

I have seen a lot of players who are so concerned with their hip turn they forget that swinging the golf club is the main point. Just remember the turn is a natural movement of the body, and your bones are connected from the ground up.

Instant Humility

In our hotel room I was nervously going over my notes for the lecture I was to present in a few hours to a large audience of my peers at a PGA convention.

I was starting to feel a little impressed with myself. Here I was, a humble growing caddie, about to give a speech on how to teach golf to a room crowded with the best golf teachers in the world.

"Just consider it, Helen," I said. "Of all the great teachers, they have chosen me to make this talk. How many great teachers do you suppose will be there?"

My lovely wife looked up from the book she was reading.

"I don't know how many great teachers will be there, Harvey," she said. "But it's probably one less than you think."

Maxims

In 1943 Jack Burke, Sr., compiled a list of golf maxims that grew out of discussions with players and teachers, one of whom was me.

1. The wrists play very little part in golf. The crossing of the forearms puts the punch in the golf shot.
2. The face of the club going off the line produces more poor shots than anything I know of.
3. If the club goes back properly there isn't much chance of a bad shot. *(I can't go along with this. For one thing, Jack taught an inside-out swing. I like a swing that is inside-square-inside. What Jack calls taking the club back properly means different things to different people. And many mistakes are made starting down from the top of the backswing. But I agree that if you start the club back properly, you are way ahead. What is proper for you is just to start the club back with your turn.)*
4. Split the ball in half in your mind and play the inside half; the outer half shouldn't be entertained. *(This is too much to think about. Just hit it.)*
5. Learn to pick the ball clean—don't hoe it.
6. Picture a shot going perfectly to the line.

7. If the hands are joined together as one unit, you would be surprised the amount of relaxation attained.
8. Knock the peg from under the ball. This helps to get the club straight through. (I use this image constantly in my teaching—just clip off the tee with your swing.)
9. Let the ball get in the way of the swing instead of making the ball the object.
10. Don't try to pick the ball up—the club is built for that purpose.
11. Hitting behind the ball is caused by the weight being on the back foot. If the weight is forward it is impossible to hit behind the ball.
12. The reason for not going forward is tenseness—keep the hands together, then the move forward is easy.
13. Picture the shot as you would *like* to see it.
14. Keep your feet moving to the line of flight. Don't let them freeze to the ground.
15. The shank shot is caused by the club being on the outside of the ball. The heart stops but the mouth doesn't. Put two balls together two inches apart; if you can miss the outside ball, the shank shot is cured. *(I don't agree with the cause and have more to say about this in my remarks on the shank.)*
16. Have a little power left—don't put it all in the swing. You may need it before the game is over.
17. Let the club go where you expect the ball to.
18. Finishing the swing is very important. Without a good finish, to keep the ball straight is luck.
19. Get a system of some kind in playing. Any kind of a system beats trusting to luck.
20. Topping the ball is caused by closing the face of

the club toward the body. *(I think more often topping the ball is caused by stiffening the knees.)*
21. Slicing is caused by the hands leading the head of the club. Tenseness plays a major part. The face of the club is not flush at impact.
22. Anyone slicing the ball has reached the top of his game. The harder he hits it, the more it will slice.
23. A ball lying badly, better try to pick it in preference to hoeing it out.
24. Be honest with yourself. What you would find out in six months of practice, your pro can tell you in five minutes.
25. Hit the ball, then the ground—that will assure you of getting down to the ball.
26. Let the right hip take the club back and the left hip bring the club forward.
27. Try holding your right shoulder back as long as possible to give your left side a chance to get through.
28. Hold the head of the club off the ground if you are inclined to be tense.
29. Let the hands start slightly before the head of the club on the backswing.

The Mythical Perfect Swing

HERE IS HOW to make the Mythical Perfect Swing that all golfers are always pursuing:

Stand a few paces behind the ball and look down the line toward the target.

Walk to the ball from behind, get a good grip, pass the club back of the ball square to the target, then adjust your stance to fit.

Have a slight waggle and then set the club back of the ball again and make a forward press similar to what you would do swinging a bucket of water.

In the first move back as the club gets parallel to the ground, the toe of the club points directly up, and the left heel starts off the ground.

Let the club come on up, keeping your elbows in front of your body, to the top of your backswing, where the clubhead will be pointing almost to the ground.

Return your left heel to the ground and simultaneously let your right elbow move back to your side as it comes down.

Weight has started shifting to your left side. Your forearms cross over as they swing. Your head stays behind the ball, perhaps even moving slightly more behind it.

Finish with your forearms in front of you. A good finish shows what has gone before it. Let your head come up to look at the good shot.

On your follow-through, the right foot merely helps to hold your balance.

If you have lost your balance during this Mythical Perfect Swing, it is probably because your grip is too weak or too tight or both.

Practice this at home in slow motion without a ball.

Be sure you don't watch the clubhead go back. Swing the clubhead at a spot every time.

Force yourself to approach the ball from behind before every swing, even on the carpet.

Make ten to twenty Mythical Perfect Swings each night, teaching your muscles what your brain wants.

Using a weighted club during this exercise can be even more beneficial.

First Things First

A NEW YORKER showed up at Austin Country Club one day. He said he'd heard about this famous teacher, this Penick fellow.

I asked, "What can I do for you?"

"If you're such a great teacher, teach me how to get out of sand traps," the New Yorker said.

"Not so fast," I said. "I can teach you how to get out of sand traps. But I'm not going to do it until I teach you how to avoid getting into them in the first place."

The Prettiest Swing

THE PRETTIEST SWING I ever saw belonged to MacDonald Smith.

Smith was born in Carnoustie and learned to play golf in Scotland.

In 1926 Smith won the Texas Open, Dallas Open, Metropolitan Open, and Chicago Open. I was flirting with playing on the tour in those days and was fortunate to know and watch Smith in his peak years.

His swing was full and flowing and graceful. I wouldn't know how else to describe it. It didn't break down into parts any more than a wonderful poem breaks down into words.

After 1926 Smith went on to win enough tournaments to be named to the PGA Hall of Fame. But in the ten years after the Dallas Open, he never won again in Texas.

The reason is that the Great Depression hit and our Texas courses received even less water than they had been accustomed to, which was very little.

This left us playing off of bare lies, and we had to hit down on our iron shots. But Smith didn't hit down on the ball. He swept it away without a divot.

At clinics Smith would hit full 2-irons off the putting green and there would be only a brushing of the grass.

They used to say he could hit the ball off an altar cloth without disturbing it.

You couldn't swing that way and win on the Texas courses.

Smith told me what happened to him on the last round of a British Open. They played 36 holes on the final day, and at lunch Smith was leading and the bookies made him a 5–1 favorite.

In the afternoon round, Smith told me, he kept getting bad lies or finding his ball on a trampled piece of ground. He realized what was happening. The bookies were running along ahead of him making sure he didn't have any luck.

Bobby Jones passed him and won the championship.

Hitting the Target

OVER THE YEARS I was a main drawing card at golf clinics and PGA schools.

At one PGA school I was demonstrating how to hit an iron shot out of a fairway sand trap. With a 4-iron I took dead aim at a tree 185 yards away. My shot landed four feet from the target.

"Can you do that with a wood?" someone asked.

I had seldom tried this shot with a wood. But I accepted the challenge.

I made my swing and heard a voice in the background say, "He not only hit the tree—he went through an opening in the branches."

The Magic Move

If there is any such thing as a Magic Move in the golf swing, to me it is an action that I stress over and over on the practice tee and in this book.

You have heard it from me many times by now, but I will say it again—*to start your downswing, let your weight shift to your left foot while bringing your right elbow back down to your body.*

This is one move, not two.

Practice this move again and again. You don't need a golf club to do it. Practice until you get the feeling and rhythm of it, and then keep on practicing. Be sure your eyes are trained on the spot where the ball would be. Your head will stay well back.

I've read books and magazines that offered the "secret" of The Move. The secret takes different forms for different players. For Ben Hogan the move is *pronating*. For Byron Nelson the move is *a lateral shift and not pronating*.

There really is no one Magic Move.

But when you learn the *left foot-right elbow* move I have described above, you will hit the ball as if it is magic.

How to Practice the Full Swing

CHOOSE A 7-IRON or a 6-iron, whichever one you feel the most confidence in, and use it for 80 percent of all your full-swing practice.

The reason for this is I want you to develop faith in your golf swing.

The best way to learn to trust your swing is by practicing your swing with a club you trust.

A high handicapper who learns to hit a good 7-iron can build his or her game around that shot. Even if you have to hit the ball twice on a par four to come within range of your 7-iron, it's a great help to know for sure that your 7-iron shot will land on the green. This will give you a putt at par even though the first two shots might have been poor efforts.

A full 7-iron swing is just about as long as a driver swing. It's the difference in length and the lie of the clubs that makes the driver swing look longer at the top of the backswing.

The main difference in swinging a 7-iron and a driver is that you want to hit your driver slightly on the upswing, or at the lowest point of the swing, and this is a function of ball position.

Some teachers have their students practice with a

3-iron on the theory that if the student can learn to hit a 3-iron, the rest of the clubs will seem easy.

This is certainly true, but it seems backward to me. It is much easier to learn to hit a good 7-iron, and that in turn will make the 3-iron easier to hit if you just use your good 7-iron swing on it.

Remember that because the number on the iron is lower does not mean you should swing the club harder.

Certainly you must practice a little with every club. But don't devote too much time to the driver. The driver is the most difficult club to hit, which is why they let you put the ball on a peg. The idea of practice is to improve—or at least to hold your own—and the surest way to do this is by practicing with a club that gives you good results.

I hate to see a high handicapper practicing the driver. It gets very ugly. The golfer becomes frustrated, and the swing gets worse and worse. Most high handicappers or once-a-week players should lock the driver in a closet and practice and play with a 3-wood.

If the average golfer hits the 3-wood off the tee, the shots will on the whole be more successful. What you will miss is maybe that one good driver shot in a round, and it's not worth it.

Warming Up in a Hurry

IF YOU ARRIVE at the course with just a few minutes to warm up before a round, use that time to hit chip shots.

The chip shot, being a short version of the full swing, tells your muscles and your golfing brain to get ready to play.

Most average golfers with only a few minutes to warm up will rush to the range and try to hit balls fast. This may loosen up the grease, but it also can ruin your tempo for the day and perhaps implant negative thoughts.

Some average golfers think they are wiser because they rush to the putting green instead, and try to hit as many putts as possible before being called to the tee. This is just as bad as rushing on the range. You'll probably miss a lot of those putts you're in such a hurry to hit, and by the time you tee off you will be doubting your putting ability.

To warm up in a hurry and arouse your sense of feel or touch, use the time you have to stroke a few careful chip shots.

This will put your mind on the business at hand— which is to play golf. If your mind is still back at the office when you go to the first tee, you are in for a rough day.

Chipping

THE FIRST AND foremost fundamental to learn about chipping is this: keep your hands ahead of or even with the clubhead on the follow-through. All the way through.

Grip your club down close to the steel. Flex your knees so you can get down to it. Keep the club near to you, instead of reaching out for the ball. Move your weight a little more to your left foot.

Loosen your elbows. Remember that you are hitting the ball with your hands, not with your elbows.

Make your backswing and your follow-through approximately the same length, as in the putting stroke.

Use the straightest-faced club that will carry the ball onto the green the soonest and start it rolling toward the cup.

Off a downhill lie or a tight lie or into the wind or with a fast green, always choose to chip the ball rather than pitch it.

Under pressure around the green, always go to the straightest blade that will do the job. It may require a 3-iron to get the roll you need.

High handicappers should use their putters from off the green whenever it looks feasible. They'll generally get closer to the hole this way.

Putting

Just as in chipping, the first and foremost fundamental to learn about the putting stroke is: keep the hands even with or ahead of the head of the putter on the follow-through.

There are many great putters—like Billy Casper and Chi Chi Rodriguez—who use a wristy stroke and pop the ball as the clubhead passes their hands.

If I see a student using that sort of stroke and making a lot of putts, I won't try to change it. Putting is an individual matter. Bobby Locke hooked his putts. I would never try to teach a student to putt that way, but I sure wouldn't try to make Bobby Locke stop it.

The way I teach you to putt is by using a simple system.

Read your line from behind the ball. Walk to the ball from behind and take your stance with your hands slightly ahead of the ball or straight up. Glance at the hole and glance at your putter blade to make sure it is square to your line.

Now take one, two or three practice strokes, concentrating on each one as if you are trying to make the putt, judging the distance. I like to see the stroke start with a small forward press, using the swing-the-bucket image.

Then put your putter blade down behind the ball, keep your head and eyes still, and imitate your last practice stroke.

One great value to this system is that it puts your mind on the stroke and not on the importance of the putt. Never—I repeat, never—allow yourself to think about what is riding on the putt, whether it's a major championship or just a 50-cent wager. Hit the putt as you have hit 10,000 putts in the past. Concentrate on imitating your final practice stroke, not on what will happen if you either miss it or make it.

When practicing putting, always choose a level place on the green, or perhaps one that is slightly uphill.

I hate the old saying "never up, never in."

It's true that a ball that never reaches the cup never goes in, but neither does a ball that goes past it.

I like a putt to die at the hole. A putt that dies at the hole will sometimes topple in, whereas a putt that is struck too hard will hit the hole and spin away. Just as many putts are missed behind the hole as short of it.

The cup is only one inch wide for a putt that is struck too hard. The cup is four inches wide for a ball that dies at the hole.

Furthermore, it is much easier to sink a putt when you've left it a foot short than when you've gone three feet past, especially if it is uphill from the cup.

The main reason a putt is left short is not that you hit the putt too softly, it's that you didn't hit it squarely on the sweet spot.

I like to see a putt slip into the hole like a mouse.

One thing all great putters have in common, regardless of their style, is that the putting stroke is approximately the same length back and through.

Try to keep the putter low to the ground, but don't give up a good stroke to do it artificially.

With short putts, concentrate on the line.

With long putts, concentrate on the distance.

I prefer a putting stroke that uses the arms and wrists. But on a very long putt, you will need to use your shoulders and take a longer backswing and follow-through.

Play the ball off the left heel. Place your feet square to the line.

If you are taking the putter too much outside the line, your weight could be on your toes and your eyes might not be over the ball.

There are two reliable ways to be sure your eyes are over the ball. Either hold a ball at eye level and then drop it and see where it lands, or else hold your putter shaft straight down from eye level to the ball.

To take your grip, put your left hand on the putter the way the manufacturer designed the grip to be held. Most great putters have their right hand under a little and keep the blade square because they offset it by weakening the left hand.

Once you adopt a good system for putting, the rest of it is mental. Stay with your system.

I was at the Masters watching them play, and I noticed Jacky Cupit on the practice green. I watched him awhile and finally couldn't stand it. I walked over and said, "Jacky, would you mind if I make a suggestion?"

He said, "Why do you think I've been staying close to the rope all this time?"

He had been hitting a pulled hook with his putter. Trying to correct it, he had yanked his hands way up high. I said, "Son, let's try holding that putter the way the man who made the grip intended for you to hold it. Just make your hands fit it."

Jacky went out and shot a 67, low round of the day until Ben Hogan came in with a 66. Jacky showed me his scorecard with a happy grin and said, "Harvey, we did it!" I hadn't really done anything except give him a positive thought.

I hear people talk about hitting putts with overspin. I say this is nearly impossible. It's like in shooting pool; to put overspin on a pool ball, you have to hit it with the cue tip on the top seven tenths of the ball. You don't want to try to hit a putt like that.

A good putt dies out straight. A bad putt slithers away.

Be decisive on the putting green. Decide what you want to do on a putt and then do it with confidence, even if it should prove to be wrong.

You should make it a habit to carry your putter in your left hand. Or in both hands, if you wish. But never carry it in your right hand alone.

Your left hand and arm are an extension of the putter shaft. That is the feeling you want to have.

I see pros on the tour place the putter behind the ball with their right hand. Then when they put their left hand on the club, they have automatically changed their aim.

Put your putter behind the ball with your left hand, or with both hands.

Think positively.

The reason I am so hipped on putting is two of my best friends were the best putters of their time—Horton Smith and Ben Crenshaw.

Horton Smith used a practice putting drill that I recommend. Stroke a few putts using only your right hand. When you get the feeling for it, allow your left hand to join in gently. But I like both hands to work together.

A good drill for developing touch is to putt a ball 30 feet. Then putt the next one 29 feet. Then 28 feet, and so on.

Play games on the putting green. The more time you spend there, the better golf scores you will turn in.

The Dreaded Four-Footer

A WOMAN AT CHURCH remarked to me, "Harvey, that game you play doesn't make sense. You hit a ball 250 yards off the tee and it counts one stroke, the same as for a three- or four-foot putt."

Not even the most expert of golfers would argue the point with her. At his home club, Shady Oaks in Fort Worth, Ben Hogan likes to play fairways and greens and closest to the pin, leaving out putting entirely.

Orville Moody said the four-foot putt almost ran him off the tour. "I just can't get over the fact that I can hit two great shots covering maybe 440 yards, and be four feet from the cup, and if I miss that little-bitty putt it counts as much as the two great shots," he said.

This was before Orville got his extra-long putter and started winning big money on the Senior Tour. (Being old-fashioned, I don't like the extra-long putters. They look funny to me. I think there should be a rule in golf that the two hands must touch each other.)

One of the 85-shooters at my club told me, "Harvey, I'd rather face a 175-yard carry across a lake than a four-foot putt."

Teaching seminars I would often start by saying, "Getting up in front of you teaching professionals makes me more nervous than anything except a three-foot downhill putt that breaks to the left on a slick green."

(Upon reading that statement, many of you are probably saying, "Harvey got it backward. Everybody knows a downhill putt that breaks to the right is the hardest putt for a righthander."

Just let me say that in many years of conducting seminars for up to 250 pros in a class, not a one of them ever argued with me about the left-breaking downhill putt causing their nerves to get jumpy.

The fact is that both the left- and right-breakers are very difficult. The reason I say the left-breaker is hardest is that you aim to the right of the hole and your stroke tends to come from the inside, hooking the ball through the break.)

Let's think a moment about these dreaded short putts and see if we can remove some of the fear.

An average golfer misses short putts because of fear or a lack of concentration. Instead of thinking about stroking the putt into the hole, he or she is thinking about any number of things—including the other players who are standing on the green watching for the result.

The average player usually doesn't work as hard lining up a three- or four-footer as lining up a ten-footer that might be an easier putt.

Another major mistake I see in average golfers is that they try to guide the short putt into the hole. They try to use their stroke to steer the ball through the break.

The right way to do it is to approach the short putt from behind and line it up. If you decide it breaks two inches left of the cup then that's where you want to stroke it—not jerk it toward the hole.

Use the system. Make one, two or three practice

strokes, concentrating on the line, washing bad thoughts out of your mind. Then imitate your last practice stroke. Don't look up and peek at it. Just stroke it on the line. This routine helps to keep your thoughts from being distracted.

Negative thoughts and carelessness cause more missed short putts than any other factor.

If it's a downhill putt that breaks to the left, an aspirin is to stroke the ball on the toe of the putter. This removes some or all of the break.

When I tell students this, they always ask, "Does that mean I should hit the putt on the heel if it breaks the other way?"

My answer is no. Never hit it on the heel.

A three- or four-footer that is straight will always go in if you stroke the ball in the sweet spot on the putter face, provided you are aimed at the center of the cup.

Don't worry about anything but the line. You'll hit the ball hard enough.

Be careful in lining up the short ones. Use the system and believe in what you're doing.

The greatest players in the world miss short putts, but not very often. There's no reason you should miss them, either.

The Shank Shot

A SHANK SHOT is so ugly that I hate to write the word.

Let's call it a Lateral Shot instead.

I had a student, a good player, who started hitting these Lateral Shots all of a sudden. He called me to the range and showed me.

Knowing he was a good player and thinking he would work his own way out of it, I said, "I'll bet you can't do that twelve times in a row."

So he stood there and did it twelve times in a row.

"Now what?" he said.

"Go home and come back tomorrow," I said.

Most people think this shot is caused by hitting the ball with a closed blade at impact, but this is improbable. Usually the shot is caused by blocking off a pull, or what you think is going to be a pull.

The ball may be too far forward. Beginners may be standing too close to it. Experienced players may be standing too far back.

Many times it is caused by the player trying to hold his or her head down too much. This drops the head way down and extends the arc of the club, resulting in a bent left arm at impact.

Or it can be caused by poor eyesight. Any pilot will tell you eyesight will change a bit from day to day.

Cures for the Lateral Shot:

Try conscientiously to hit every iron shot on the toe of the club until you stop shanking.

Never aim to the left. You would do well to think you are aimed to the right.

Feel like the toe of the club is rolling over.

Place a pasteboard box or a tee about one inch outside of the ball lined up at the target. Hit the ball without hitting the box or the tee.

It is almost impossible to hit a Lateral Shot if the blade is closed. Try it sometime. Close the blade and make your best swing and follow through. Keep it closed throughout the swing. The ball may go to the left—but I don't think you can hit it laterally.

Why I Decided to Become a Teacher

SAM SNEAD.

I thought I was a pretty fair player and had nagging aspirations to join the tour until a Houston Open in the middle 1930's.

I was practicing putting and one of the fellows said, "Harvey, have you seen this kid Snead hit the ball? He's about to tee off now."

I walked over to the tee and saw the new kid from West Virginia hit his drive. I not only saw it, I heard it.

It sounded like a rifle and the ball flew like a bullet.

I knew right that moment that my future was not as a tour player.

The Stance

FACE THE BALL plain, as if you are about to shake hands with someone on the other side of it. There's no need to get your body twisted into some kind of funny shape. If you were going to shake hands with someone, you wouldn't bend sideways or slump sharply forward like so many beginners do.

If you are slew-footed by nature, it's better to point your toes out the way you walk. If you are pigeon-toed, you'll want your feet more square.

The Hogan foot position is preferred by many good players. This has the right foot square to the line and the left foot turned toward the target a few inches. The advantage of this is that the square right foot helps shorten a too-long backswing, and the slanted left foot helps to make a full weight shift and follow-through.

The average golfer may want the right foot toed out slightly to allow for more turn.

If you want to close your stance, pull your right foot back a few inches from the line. But be sure you turn your hips and shoulders to fit it. So many average golfers think if they just pull back the right foot, they have closed their stance. In fact, if they pull back the right foot but leave the hips and shoulders square, they haven't made any change at all.

To open your stance, pull your left foot back a few inches from the line and let your hips and shoulders go with it.

When you stand to the ball, just flex the knees a little, as if you are making the first move toward sitting down. When I tell students to flex the knees, so often they start jiggling up and down, which looks very amateurish.

I am careful about using this "sitting-down" thought, because the next time I see the student he or she may have swallowed the whole bottle of medicine and really be in a posture that looks like sitting in a chair.

Be comfortable and at ease, not straining anything.

Wesley Ellis, Jr., who played for me in college before he went on the tour, had the most natural-looking stance I ever saw. Wesley just walked up to the ball in his normal stride, stopped and hit it. He kept the ball in play more than anyone I know of.

Wesley used to have a dog that would follow him faithfully on rounds of golf at Brackenridge Park. The dog would sit quietly, never bothering anyone. What a fine companion.

A Very Bad Habit

WATCHING THE CLUBHEAD go back as you start your swing will probably ruin any chance you have of hitting a good shot.

Anything you do wrong taking the clubhead back is not as bad as watching it.

It is amazing how many golfers get into this habit.

The First-Time Student

Before I take a student onto the range, I like to go into the clubhouse for a cup of coffee and a chat.

Usually students are nervous. I want to put them at ease. I want to gain their confidence. I ask about their game, how often they play or practice, what their goals are.

I tell them, "Any mistakes that are made out there today are mine, not yours."

When I hear one of my students griping about how his clubs are no good, I like to say, "Hey, your swings are my fault first of all, your fault second and the club maybe third."

I'll ask the new student if he or she would rather hit woods or irons, are there any aches or pains, how is life going. I want to understand my students and put them at ease with me.

This takes about twenty minutes, and it gets us off on the right foot.

Competition

BEN CRENSHAW AND Tom Kite were fortunate to grow up in the same town at the same time and attend the University of Texas together, because this gave each of them a top-quality rival from an early age.

You don't learn how to play good golf by beating poor players. In the case of Crenshaw and Kite, it was learning to play great golf against another great golfer in the same town representing competing high schools.

Ben Hogan and Byron Nelson had much the same thing going for them. They grew up at the same time in Fort Worth, and both of them caddied at Glen Garden. As a kid each of them knew who his top rival was.

As Byron and Ben grew into young men, they discovered they had a third rival—Jimmy Demaret, a kid from Houston.

In competition you must be yourself. Younger kids from Houston used to copy Demaret, who was always joking and loose. In Fort Worth, the kids would copy the seriousness of Hogan or the seemingly unemotional ways of Nelson. If you're the joking sort, go ahead and joke. If you're the serious sort, there's no need to pretend not to be.

In college I never coached a great athlete, except for Ben Crenshaw. George Hannon replaced me when I retired from coaching as Ben began to play for the University, but I still felt like his coach. Ben could play any sport with success. I was so happy to see him give up the others and choose golf.

Most of the college golfers in my coaching career were not athletes capable of making the team in any big-time varsity sport except golf. One of my best college players of all time, Morris Williams, Jr., who would have become a champion on the pro tour had he not been killed flying a jet fighter in 1954, couldn't even swim.

As the purses grew rich on the tour, better athletes began to play college golf. Jack Nicklaus, whose first teacher, Jack Grout, was an old friend of mine from Fort Worth, could have excelled in several sports.

And today I look at TV and see players like the young PGA champion, John Daly, and I know he could play other sports. There are pros who are big-muscle swingers and some who are arm swingers, but Daly is both. Many well-meaning people will try to change Daly's extremely long, across-the-line swing. But from what I have seen of him, I wouldn't change much.

Because a golfer might not be an athlete doesn't mean he or she won't be a top competitor. Pool hustlers are great competitors.

When football players come to me for lessons, I find that ends and quarterbacks make the best players as a rule. The hardest to teach are the big, muscle-bound boys. Earl Campbell, the powerful Heisman Trophy running back at Texas, plays a lot of golf, but he has never come to me for a lesson.

If he does, I'll set him to practicing his short game.

I compare the pressure of a golf shot with making an extra point in basketball. The player starts from a full stop, and that rim doesn't move.

Visiting with basketball coaches, I ask what they tell their players before a crucial free throw with the game on the line. Most coaches say they tell the player, "Be yourself."

In golf, I need to know the player well before I can give advice on how to respond under pressure of a big match. Some do their best when they know the pressure is on, and some do better if I can keep them from thinking about it.

Kids and Carts

In my opinion, no young player can develop his or her game to its highest potential if he or she rides around the course in a golf cart.

If they are old enough to swing a club, they should be walking, strengthening their legs, learning to feel the rhythm of the game that simply cannot be learned in a golf cart.

It's all right for youngsters to ride on a cart with Dad or Mom and have fun. But four youngsters driving around the course in two carts is a sad sight.

Walter Hagen said to stop and smell the flowers while you're on the course. This sensitivity is a powerfully alluring and educational part of golf. You're much less likely to realize it if you grow up riding in a cart.

A Story by Helen

When we got married sixty years ago, Harvey already had a big reputation in golf. He became head pro at Austin Country Club at 18 and golf coach at Texas at 26. So I was always known as Mrs. Harvey Penick. Only our friends knew me as Helen.

People would say, "She's Mrs. Harvey Penick. She's bound to know how to play golf." I loved the game, but I was an 18-handicapper. I finally started using my maiden name—Helen Holmes—when I would enter a tournament.

The last time I played with Harvey was in a Scotch Foursome at the old Austin Country Club on Riverside Drive. We were matched against Martha and Peck Westmoreland from Lockhart.

Before we teed off, Harvey told me, "Helen, Peck is hitting the ball so bad. It's his grip. Would you mind riding in the cart with Martha while I see if I can help Peck?"

After six holes, Peck was playing very well. Harvey came to me and said, "Helen, Martha is having a terrible time with her putting stroke. Would you ride with Peck for a while, and I'll try to help Martha."

Martha took two putts on the seventh and one-putted the eighth and ninth.

On the tenth tee I said, "Harvey, you helped Martha and Peck. Now tell me what I am doing wrong."

Harvey said, "I don't know. I haven't been looking."

So I quit playing with him.

He used to give me a fifteen-minute lesson and then go hide.

But maybe that's one reason we've stayed married so long.

Learning

I LEARN TEACHING from teachers.

I learn golf from golfers.

I learn winning from coaches.

There are many good teachers of golf who teach quite differently from each other. I prefer listening to one who teaches differently than I do. I might learn from him. I already know my own way.

The piano master Horowitz told his students, "Never be afraid to dare. Never be afraid to play without asking advice. I'm not going to teach you, but to guide you."

I read that quote to Tinsley, and he said, "Why, that sounds just like you."

I'll always remember what my cousin, Dr. D.A. Penick, said when he turned over the reins as University of Texas tennis coach to Wilmer Allison:

"Wilmer, I know you'll make better players of your students in four years. But will they be better people? That's the important thing."

Some of the Women in My Life

I HAVE BEEN lucky to coach and teach the winners of ten U.S. Women's Opens and four of the twelve players who are in the LPGA Hall of Fame—the most exclusive Hall of Fame in sports.

I am very proud of them and of many other excellent women students I have been able to guide in my career.

But there is no teaching I am more proud of than what I was able to do with the woman who flew from Paris to see me.

THE WOMAN FROM PARIS

She was a small, pretty, dark-eyed woman who had no natural ability at all for golf.

I don't think she had ever hit anything with a stick in her life.

When I asked where she was from, she said, "Paris." I said, "Paris, Texas?" She said, "No. Paris, France."

I was amazed that she had come all the way from France to take lessons and couldn't even hit the ball off the ground.

Visiting with her before the first lesson, I asked what

her goal was, and she said she wanted to be able to play golf with her husband by the time she went home.

She hit at a few balls without a clue as to how to swing a club.

I stood in front of her and took hold of the shaft of the club, with her hands on the grip. I started her backswing motion by moving the shaft straight back until it was parallel to the ground and told her to go with me. Now my hand moved the club straight up, and she naturally turned and lifted her left heel off the ground.

I started the club handle pulling down. The left heel naturally planted on the ground again. I swung the shaft very slowly on through to the finish, with her elbows in front.

Then I did it again and again. Five times.

Each time I added a little more rhythm, getting her into the swing-the-bucket image without telling her.

"Now you know how to do it," I said.

I teed up a ball.

"Just swing the club like you know how," I said. "I don't want you to feel like you are going to hit a golf ball. I want you to cut that tee off with your swing."

This pretty little woman hit the ball up in the air and it carried 75 yards.

I don't know who was happier, the student or the teacher. She jumped up and kissed me. "I'm so thrilled!" she said.

She stayed for a week. Every day I gave her a lesson.

When she could hit the ball pretty well, I told her, "You're ready to go play golf with your husband now. The first five times you play with him, put the ball on a tee for every shot, so you won't try to help it up. After that, you'll be really playing golf."

She went back to France and turned into a fair player

and enjoyed the game with her husband for many years.

What more could a teacher ask?

BETTY JAMESON

My first woman student to become famous was Betty Jameson. She came to the University of Texas at age 19 with a good amateur record behind her. Betty is quite a character. She's an excellent painter, loves the arts. Helen used to go pick Betty up at the dorm, bring her to me for lessons and then take her home again.

Betty had some good help from Tod Menefee in San Antonio and from Francis Scheider in Dallas, where she really started playing.

When she came to me, she had a tendency to pull her iron shots to the left. We practiced getting her left side and left arm under control. She won big amateur tournaments like the Trans-Miss and the Texas Amateur. In the state amateur, she was six down at noon in the 36-hole finals. She phoned her "good luck friend" in San Antonio and asked her to drive to Austin in a hurry. Her friend arrived in time, and Betty won the state amateur.

Betty left school at the age of 21 and joined the tour, where she won the U.S. Women's Open twice and made the Hall of Fame.

Betty and I were named to the Texas Sports Hall of Fame together, a big thrill for me. She is now an artist in Florida.

KATHY WHITWORTH

Kathy Whitworth is one of the sweetest and most thoughtful people I ever knew. Hardy Loudermilk, the pro in Jal, New Mexico, called and said he was sending her to me. Kathy's mother drove her 500 miles to Austin.

When Kathy arrived, she weighed 175 pounds. It looked like her favorite sport was ice box.

I encouraged her to lose weight and gave her a better grip and follow-through. She went back and won the New Mexico Amateur and enrolled in junior college. But she dropped out of school in a few months. She wrote me a letter that said, "I guess you'll want to kick me in the seat of the pants, but I want to go on the pro tour." Her mother drove her to Beaumont, where Kathy finished in the money in her first tournament.

Kathy has won more tournaments than any other player, man or woman, including Sam Snead.

She makes more long putts when she needs them than any other player I ever saw.

Kathy was visiting Helen and me recently while I gave her lessons on how to teach. Many great players like Kathy make the swing in a way that is natural to them. They don't have to think about it or explain it.

I put Kathy through my discussion on The Turn. She was pleased to learn how to put this action into simple words. Many great players can show you their beautiful swing, but they can't tell you how they do it.

"Harvey, you built my swing from the ground up, and you never in my life mentioned the shoulder turn to me until right how," she said. "Why is that?"

I said, "Kathy, you already had a good natural shoulder turn. You didn't need to hear about it."

The U.S. Women's Open is about the only thing Kathy never won. But she made the LPGA Hall of Fame without it. There's no nicer person on earth than Kathy. She's going to be a famous teacher.

BETSY RAWLS

Betsy Rawls came to the University of Texas out of high school with a very strong grip. She was a talented player who loved golf, and I began gradually to change her grip. Betsy improved fast and won the city tournament in Austin, followed by the state championship.

I taught her that she must learn to play on all kinds of courses—good and bad—with all different sorts of people. I learned a lot from Betsy in return. She was a Phi Beta Kappa in physics.

One thing I learned from Betsy was that you don't win a tournament with good golf shots only. There are many more things of importance, and they grow even more important when you start playing against the whole world.

Betsy could choose a club and have confidence it was right with no indecision. The same applied once she decided on the type of shot—pitch or chip, hook or fade, whatever.

She knew the person in the best physical shape had the advantage, especially on the last day of a tournament. She kept herself in top shape, always ate a healthy and correct diet.

Betsy had the ability to walk over and say hello to someone in the gallery and then return to her shot with total concentration. We discussed whether it was best for me as coach to apply pressure, or just let the player know I was interested in improvement, and I took her advice, in relation to other players I coached as well as Betsy herself.

I learned from Betsy not to give a pupil too many things to think about in one lesson. One day I was teaching her two or three things at once. She said, "Harvey, let's learn one or two things this week and save the third thing for next week."

That was a real lesson for me. If a Phi Beta Kappa and talented golfer like Betsy can't concentrate on more than two things at once, what chance would an ordinary student have?

This became a cornerstone of my teaching—one thing at a time.

The only times Betsy would get off her game, she would start hitting a right-to-right push shot. But we always worked it out.

Betsy won four U.S. Women's Opens and made the Hall of Fame.

A major intercollegiate women's tournament, named for her, is played every year in Austin with entrants from all over the country.

She was an ideal pupil. She had good common sense and the willpower to make any shot that was important, whether it was a drive or a putt.

MICKEY WRIGHT

Mickey Wright was already a fine player when she came to me. Mickey was on the tour, but she wasn't winning. I didn't dare to change her swing. It was too good. She had learned the Alex Morrison style in California.

Mickey felt she should never miss a shot. I tried to help her realize that we are all human and not to be too tough on herself. Her favorite pastime was to go to Fort Worth and sit and watch Ben Hogan practice. She asked Hogan if he minded. He replied, "Not as long as you don't say anything."

She won three U.S. Women's Opens and made the

Hall of Fame. Surely Mickey is the greatest woman player of all time.

Mickey had a little different left heel than most fine swingers. She turned on the inside of her left foot, a la Alex Morrison.

Mickey was a "lively-handed" player, my favorite type. Players with lively hands, who can whip that club through the ball, are not seen so often anymore. Among men, Don January, Ray Mangrum and Chi Chi Rodriquez are the most lively-handed I ever saw. Among women, Mickey was tops, and Kathy Whitworth was close.

I love to watch lively-handed golfers deal cards and see those fingers flip and flash.

Some would say Babe Didrickson Zaharias was the best woman golfer ever, but my money is on Mickey. Mickey had all the shots. She could shoot a 62 in the wind on a good golf course.

It's a thrill for me to remember Mickey and that beautiful swing of hers.

A few years ago Mickey and Kathy teamed up against the men in the Legends of Golf Senior Tournament in Austin and were very popular with the galleries, but the men pros didn't like the competition and they weren't invited back.

The first time I saw Mickey swing a club, I asked her, "Where did you get that wonderful follow-through?"

She pulled an elastic loop out of her bag and showed me how she practiced with the loop around her elbows, keeping them close together.

The first person I ever saw use an elastic loop was Abe Mitchell, a long-hitting Englishman in the late 1920's and early 1930's.

This is an excellent training aid. If you should go to

Broadmoor in Colorado and take a lesson from the superb teacher Mary Lena Faulk, one of my best students, I'll bet she puts an elastic loop around your elbows.

Anything that can help you swing like Mickey Wright is something you want to pursue.

JUDY KIMBALL

Judy Kimball Simon was a favorite pupil who still comes to see us in her own airplane from her home in North Platte, Nebraska.

She won the LPGA in Las Vegas among her many victories. Of all my women students, Judy was the best putter. For many years Judy held the LPGA record for fewest putts in an 18-hole round—19, I believe.

Often I have watched Judy and Tommy Kite putting round after round on the putting green.

Once Ben Crenshaw needed to use an airplane to scout a piece of land upon which he wanted to build a golf course in Nebraska. Ben phoned a number someone gave him and explained his problem.

"Well, Ben," a woman's voice said, "you have called the right person. I've known you since you were eight years old."

It was Judy Kimball—now Simon.

BABE DIDRICKSON ZAHARIAS

I played with Babe in her first exhibition as a professional. She and Al Espinosa, a Ryder Cup pro, were matched against the sweet-swinging Mrs. Vola Mae Odom, a club member, and me.

The Babe gave her usual show with wit and long, wild drives that entertained the gallery. I remember a shot she hit at the third hole. It was a half-topped 7-iron that hit the green and skidded across to the back. "These greens don't hold very well, do they, Harvey?" she asked, and the gallery laughed.

A Supreme Court justice was in the crowd. Babe would turn to him after a shot and say, "How'd you like that one, Judge?"

Babe always drew big galleries. I really enjoyed her. She could tell the other women, "I'm going to win this tournament," and make them like it.

She hit the consistently longest tee ball of any other woman in history until this Englishwoman, Laura Davies, came along. But Babe didn't always know where her drives were going.

She was an all-around superior athlete, just as good at track or softball or basketball as she was at golf. Babe was probably the best woman athlete who ever lived, and the second-best golfer behind Mickey Wright.

After Babe died of cancer at a tragically young age, I had a long visit in Florida with her husband, George, who had quit his career as a professional wrestler to become his wife's manager. George was deeply in love with Babe, and she with him. He wept when we talked about her.

Babe used to give me some credit for her success, but I didn't deserve any. She was a self-made player.

SANDRA PALMER, BETTY HICKS, BETTY DODD AND MORE . . .

Sandra Palmer came to me from Fort Worth on the advice of Betsy Rawls. Sandra had been a caddie and had worked in a hamburger stand. She was adopted by two fine people who were members of Glen Garden, where she started becoming a good player.

Sandra was always very popular and has a wonderful personality. She was a cheerleader and Homecoming Queen at North Texas State. Sandra was 23, teaching school in Fort Worth, when Betsy sent her to me. Sandra drove to Austin every weekend for help, rain or shine, for a whole year and stayed with Helen and me.

At first I found her backswing to be so fast it made her turn loose of the club at the top. Some teachers tell their students to hold tight with the little finger and ring finger of the left hand—which I used to teach before I decided it cuts down too much on distance. It was hard for Sandra to loosen her grip and slow her backswing, but we did it.

Going to the first tee in 1976 for her playoff with JoAnne Carner in the U.S. Women's Open, Sandra said, "Big Mama, I'm going to beat you this time." Carner said, "No, you're not, you Little Shrimp." Carner won, and the nicknames stuck.

Sandra is a big buddy of my wife Helen's and a good friend to me. I got a huge kick out of watching on television when she holed a bunker shot to win the Dinah Shore tournament. Sandra helped to dress up the women's tour. Everyone loves her.

Little Alice Ritzman, a Montana girl, was sent to me by Warren Smith, the pro at Cherry Hills in Denver. She went to work for Tinsley in our golf shop. I did everything I could imagine to get her more distance, including changing her grip to the ten-finger, and she went on the tour.

Cindy Figg-Currier is another favorite of mine. She has developed a wonderful short game and should have a great career as a professional.

One of my best pupils and nicest people was Mary Lena Faulk, who teaches golf at Broadmoor. From 175 yards, Mary Lena was the most accurate of all the women on the tour. I cut down a 5-wood for her to hit from about that distance, and she could put the ball closer to the hole with that club than others could with a 4-iron.

Betty Dodd came to me often for lessons. Her father was an Army colonel at Fort Sam Houston in San Antonio. One day the colonel was watching me with Betty on the practice tee.

I asked her, "Would you rather be known as 'sweet-swinging Betty Dodd' or as 'the long-hitting redhead?' "

"I'll answer that," Colonel Dodd said. "She wants to be the long-hitting redhead."

Betty Dodd was a pal of the Babe's. They would sing and play music together.

Betsy Rawls sent Betty Hicks to me. Betty was already a good player, who had won the U.S. Amateur. Betty had a long, loose swing and tended to lose control at the top of her backswing. When this happened, she hit a bad hook.

I told her in all good humor that she swung the club like an old cow's tail. I didn't mean to hurt her feelings, but she told me (joking, I hope) she would never forgive me.

I thought we had cured her hook until the eighth hole of a playing lesson one day when she snapped a wild one and got furious. Naturally, she followed that shot with another wild hook.

"How long have you been getting so angry?" I asked.

"Always," she said.

Betty was raised in California and played with Jackson Bradley as a youngster. After her pro playing career, she coached a golf team in San Jose, where she also teaches people how to fly airplanes. Betty is very smart. She's one of the best writers on golf I have ever read.

I've had so many fine women players as students that I can't name them all, but I remember them all fondly.

One of my most prized possessions is a wristwatch that is engraved "From Harvey's Girls." It was given to me by Betsy Rawls, Mickey Wright and Betsy Cullen, now a teaching professional in Houston.

And Some of the Men in My Life

BEN HOGAN

I was playing in a charity match in Austin with Ben Hogan, and I heard him ask his caddie, "Which way is due west?"

It was a surprise to hear Hogan ask a caddie a question. Ben thought he knew his own game better than a caddie ever could. Ben judged his own distances and pulled his own clubs.

I wondered all day why Ben had asked that question. After the round, I brought it up.

"All other things being equal, greens break to the west," Ben said.

He is right, of course. There are many reasons why, I later found out, but unless the architect has tricked up the green to fool you, your putt will break to the west.

As a young man, Ben had a very bad pull hook. He worked it out himself, getting a good grip with his right hand well on top, the V pointing to his chin.

Pronation is what he called his secret. In the hitting area, his left forearm, or possibly his entire left arm, uncoiled. This got him inside the ball and gave him a snap.

Ben practiced thousands of hours perfecting his swing. At first he felt his swing was too long. He changed his stance to shorten his swing a little by adopting what is now the famous Hogan Stance—the right foot square to the line and the left toe turned out a few inches. Each of these foot movements shortens the backswing.

I like a long swing if it is kept under control, and Ben certainly learned to do that.

Jimmy Demaret and Hogan became pals. Jimmy told me he called up Ben before the first Legends of Golf Senior Tournament and asked Hogan to be his partner.

Ben replied he wasn't playing often or well.

"Come on and let's have some old-time fun," Jimmy said.

Ben said, "No, I couldn't help you."

Jimmy said, "So what? You never did."

BYRON NELSON

Over the years Byron Nelson has sent me many students.

Byron was a self-made player, with the aid of one of Texas's most respected amateurs, J. K. Wadley of Texarkana. Wadley was a wealthy gentleman who loved the game and saw the brilliance in Byron and gave him a good job working with Don Morphy at Texarkana Country Club at a time when that course was ranked as one of the ten best in the state.

When Byron Nelson, Ben Hogan and Jimmy Demaret—all Texans—were the leading golfers in the country, I was the President of the Texas PGA. I studied their swings.

Nelson, Hogan and Demaret could drive the ball as far as Jimmy Thompson or any of the big hitters—if they wanted to. But they played within themselves and kept something in reserve.

Byron found out it helped him not to cock his wrists at the top of his backswing. He called it "not pronating." Byron said he stopped pronating in 1930 when he began playing with steel shafts. He started taking the club away square without opening the face of the club or rolling it open. Byron said when he stopped pronating, he learned to use his feet and legs to make a full swing without rolling his hands.

Byron had a lateral shift which I believe helped him in getting a thin divot that looked like a dollar bill—one of the few I ever saw in that precise shape. He felt that not pronating kept his clubface straight down the line longer.

I was always flattered that Byron kept sending me students. He thought I didn't know he was shipping me his problems, but I was honored to have the challenge.

JIMMY DEMARET

Jimmy Demaret could hit more different good shots than anyone else who ever won major championships on the tour. Only a great trick-shot artist like Joe Kirkwood could hit as many different shots as Jimmy—low, high, hook, slice, whatever he wanted.

Jimmy had the forearms of a giant and could hit that little ball in what he called a "quail shot" that didn't go more than two or three feet off the ground.

As a young pro I developed tremendously strong forearms and hands because every day I had to go through every member's bag and polish his irons with a buffer to prevent them from rusting. But I was never anywhere near as strong as Demaret.

In the winter in rainy, cold weather and hard wind, Demaret would beat anybody. He learned to play in the wind and rain at Offat's Bayou on Galveston Island as a young man.

As a young player Jimmy had as fine a swing as anyone ever. Later his swing became shorter but was always stylish. He had a good influence on my teaching. One day he casually said, "I like these kids who keep their elbows out in front of them throughout the swing," and that became one of my fundamentals.

Demaret and Walter Hagen raised the level of golf pros to one of much more respect than before they came along.

Jimmy loved to joke with people, especially serious ones like his friend Hogan. One day they were playing together, just after Ben had written an article saying you should swing a golf club as if you had a pane of glass in front of you, slanting down from the chin, to keep the swing in plane.

Ben hit a poor shot, and Jimmy said, "Hey, Ben, did you hear the sound of glass shattering?"

Jimmy looked dapper, relaxed and casual on the golf course, but don't let that fool you. He played to win.

BOBBY JONES

Bobby Jones hit the best golf shot I ever saw in a tournament. I was playing in the group 150 yards behind him at East Lake in Atlanta at the Southern Open and had a clear view.

On the seventh hole there is a big canyon on the right of the green with a grassy hollow at the bottom. The weather had been nasty, and suddenly hailstones as big as marbles began falling. The whole green was covered with hailstones. Jones had been down in the grassy hollow, but had pitched the ball just to the crown of the hill where he could hardly tell a golf ball from a hailstone. From there, he chipped the ball among the hailstones and it rolled right into the cup—for a par.

Jones had a way of doing whatever was necessary. Jack Burke, Sr., said that to win a tournament the Lord has to put His hand on your head. This happened to Jones over and over.

Bobby didn't even play golf all that much. He'd put his clubs away in the summer when it was hot and get them out just in time to practice for a major tournament, which he would frequently win. He seldom played in college.

I've always said the best golf teacher of all has to be Stewart Maiden of East Lake. He taught Jones and Glenna Collett Vare.

Stewart never gave Bobby a formal lesson. He would just come watch Jones on the practice tee and say something like, "You don't hit it with your backswing, laddie."

Bobby and his daddy both had hot tempers. They were playing together one day when daddy hit a bad shot and slammed his club on the ground. Then dad took a good practice swing and said, "What's wrong with that?"

"Nothing," Bobby said. "Try it on the ball sometime."

Bobby's famous putter, Calamity Jane, had a lot of tape and glue on the shaft because he broke it from time to time. Calamity Jane had the loft of a 2-iron, which was needed for the furry greens of those days. His putting stroke was long and smooth, like Ben Crenshaw's, but Bobby rolled the blade of the putter open and closed it during his stroke.

Like many players of the time, Bobby saw to it that his iron clubs were all red and pitted with rust on the face. This kept the ball on the face longer for more control.

Because Bobby made a number of movie shorts, his swing has been preserved on videotape and is widely studied by golfers of all levels.

He played with his feet close together, even on the long shots. That made it easier to turn, but a windy day could blow most players off balance—but not Jones.

At the top of his swing, Jones looked like he was waving a flag. People thought he turned loose of the club at the top. But he didn't. He just had a loose grip that, he said, "helped me to put some snap in the swing."

Jones had a long, smooth swing with a little loop at the top that brought the club to the ball from the inside. He was up on his toes at impact, but he kept perfect balance. He had a picture-book follow-through, with his elbows out front of his body.

"You just turn back and turn through," he said. He made the game look awfully easy.

People talk about the "relaxed" swing of Bobby Jones. But look at a photograph of Bobby's face at impact. You can see the frown of intense effort and concentration.

SAM SNEAD

Sam hit that low, bullet-type shot. If you want distance—whether it's for a shot-put, a BB gun or a cannon—you would want to launch at about a 45-degree angle. That's what most of us try to do.

But Sam hit down on the ball a little bit to get that bullet flying. For this reason, he used a driver off the tee with the loft of a brassie.

People would say Sam looked like he was aimed to the right. Playing at the Masters one time, another pro told him, "Sam, you are aimed at my caddie." Sam said, "No, I'm aimed at my own caddie."

For Sam the aim was perfect. He aimed a little to the right and hooked it.

I was trying to get Darrell Royal to play in Snead's style, but Darrell told me he was aimed too far to the right. Darrell thought he was pulling the ball. He wasn't accepting what I was saying.

But in the pro-am before the first Legends of Golf Tournament, Darrell was paired with Sam. Darrell came to me later and said, "I want to apologize. I didn't believe Sam could possibly be aimed to the right, but I stood behind him all day—and he was."

Sam had amazing agility. From a flat-footed stance he could leap and kick the ceiling.

Jimmy Thompson told me he always outdrove Snead on a still day or with the wind helping. But into the wind, Sam was in front of him every time.

Since he's the player who convinced me to become a teacher, I have always been a big fan of Sam's.

RALPH GULDAHL

For about three years in the middle 1930's, Ralph Guldahl of Cedar Crest in Dallas was probably the best player in the world, but he didn't get full credit for it with the public because he didn't have much flair and he didn't stay on top long enough.

Ralph won two U.S. Opens and three Western Opens in three years at a time when the Western was considered a major. As an amateur he played on the Walker Cup team, and as a young pro he nearly won another U.S. Open but lost it by one shot to Johnny Goodman, an amateur, after Ralph had made up five strokes on the final 18.

Ralph's swing was short and compact, and he hit the ball straight. For some reason, he never captured the public fancy with his personality or style of play, both of which were on the quiet, conservative side. Ralph didn't make many friends. I was probably as close to him as anyone. Many years later he told me I was his model when he was a young player.

After Ralph took a good head-pro job in St. Louis, his golf deteriorated. He and his wife became devoted to their racehorses.

JACK NICKLAUS

I can't take the slightest bit of credit for Jack Nicklaus, but he is the greatest player in history, so I have watched him closely.

Most anybody would have said the young Nicklaus couldn't have played well with that right elbow flying up the way it does. But he moves it back to his side as he starts down. And they'd say you can't play well lifting your left heel as much as he does, but they would be wrong. He doesn't lift it any more than Bobby Jones did, I don't believe.

Lifting the heel gives him a good turn and a comfortable position at the top.

Even though he is the best player who ever lived, young Jack, like all young pros at the time, was required to come to a PGA school taught by Byron Nelson and me. Byron and I thought he stood out head and shoulders above the fifty players in the school. Jack has no weaknesses in any department of the game.

A swing like his will last the rest of his life.

TOM KITE

Tom was a very long practicer on all phases of his game as a boy. He is an analytical person and a perfectionist. One day he asked me to watch him hit iron shots to the green. They looked perfect to me. "What's wrong with them?" I asked.

"They're flying about a foot too high," Tommy said.

Another time while playing, Tommy hit a 7-iron to four feet short of the cup. He frowned.

"What was wrong with that one?" I asked.

"I misjudged either the wind or the moisture of the green," Tom said.

I would give Tommy games to play while he practiced. I'd ask him to aim at a canister out on the practice range and draw the ball into it one time and fade it in the next. The range at our old club on Riverside Drive was beside the cart path en route to the first tee. I would stop foursomes coming by and say, "Watch this. Hey, Tommy, fade the ball into that canister." It put the pressure on him, and most of the time he hit the target.

Boys who practice a lot but seldom play don't learn to score. I made sure Tommy got off the range and onto the course as much as he needed. With his sound, compact swing and good short game, Tommy quickly picked up the real secret of golf—get your ball into the hole in a minimum number of strokes. He has a knack for scoring.

At an NCAA tournament, the University of Texas team was seven strokes behind going into the last day. Tommy started the first seven holes six under par, inspired the rest of the team and Texas won the title.

I was very happy for Tommy when he tied for the NCAA individual championship as a senior. In fact, I was doubly happy because the boy he tied with was Ben Crenshaw.

In all the years I taught them, I would never let Tommy watch me with Ben, nor Ben watch me with Tommy.

What applies to one of them does not apply to the other.

BEN CRENSHAW

Ben came to me when he was about 8 years old. We cut off a 7-iron for him. I showed him a good grip, and we went outside.

There was a green about 75 yards away. I asked Ben to tee up a ball and hit it onto the green. He did. Then I said, "Now, let's go to the green and putt the ball into the hole."

"If you wanted it in the hole, why didn't you tell me the first time?" little Ben asked.

Ben's mother was a fine piano player. He may have inherited his extraordinary sense of touch from her. His father, Charles, was a very good athlete.

His natural swing is long and smooth, using mostly the shoulders. I encouraged him to play golf to his heart's content and to practice only when guidance was needed.

Ben is such an excellent athlete. One day he was playing with three other good golfers at Horseshoe Bay on a very difficult course. With six holes to go, Ben was leading. He told the others he would play lefthanded the rest of the way. He shot those last six holes even par.

I have seen Ben on the course when it was so cold he was the only one playing. He would win a high school tournament, and then go play another round.

Ben's victory in the Masters in 1984 is one of the most popular wins of all time.

Ben's older brother, Charles, was just as talented a golfer as Ben when they were kids. But Charles starred in other sports and didn't concentrate on golf. It made me very happy when Ben gave up other sports and devoted himself to golf. Charles developed nongolf muscles, which are very difficult to overcome. He's in his forties now, and he can shoot 73 from the blue tees at Austin Country Club, no small feat.

I love Ben and Tommy like my own sons.

MORE FAVORITE SWINGS

Since the days of MacDonald Smith, my four favorite golf swings belong to:

1. Ben Crenshaw
2. Mickey Wright
3. Dave Marr
4. Al Geiberger

When I was coaching in Texas I would tell my young players to imitate the swing of Dave Marr more often than any other golfer.

I watch every bit of golf that comes on television now that I can't go around the course myself anymore. I confess that I would rather watch the Seniors than the regular tour. That's because I see better swings on the Seniors' tour. These older guys have swings that have stood the test of time.

Modern players use power.

Many of the players on the regular tour keep their left heel on the ground (some think they do and don't; the grass fools them), use the big back muscles at the expense of the arms and hands, and swing so hard their follow-through whips on around the body instead of finishing with the elbows in front.

I see some wonderful young players on the tour. But I also see many who will be doing something else for a living before too long.

The Sexes

No pretty woman can miss a single shot without a man giving her some poor advice.

A husband should never try to teach his wife to play golf or drive a car. A wife should never try to teach her husband to play bridge.

A Practice Rule

NEVER PRACTICE YOUR full swing when the wind is blowing at your back. If you're right-handed, this means the wind is left to right. The more you practice with the wind blowing left to right, the more you will be inclined to swing across the ball and hit from the top.

Ben Hogan was one of the first to realize this.

Ben would seek out a part of the course where the wind was blowing into his face, either right to left or head-on, and that's where he would practice.

If you practice into the wind, just use your regular swing. Don't try to hit it harder. And please be careful not to practice too many "punch" shots. There's no follow-through on a "punch" shot.

John Bredemus

JOHN BREDEMUS WAS a truly incredible person, and I am proud to say he became a friend of mine. I might have known John as well as anyone ever did. He was a loner who lived frugally in rooms that had more books than furniture. When he died of a heart attack in Abilene in 1946, his family back east would have nothing to do with him. John faced a pauper's grave. Murray Brooks, pro at Brackenridge Park, took up a collection from Texas PGA members to pay for John's funeral.

People came to the funeral and looked into John's casket to see if he was being buried with Jim Thorpe's gold medals. From 1913 until his death, John was known to many only as "the man who's got Jim Thorpe's gold medals."

Nobody ever found those gold medals. I may be the only person who knows what happened to them.

If John's life was a story in a movie, you wouldn't believe it.

He was born to immigrants from Luxembourg in Flint, Michigan, in 1884. John went to school in South Bend, Indiana, until his father died when John was 10. They sent John to the elite Phillips Exeter Academy in New Hampshire. He became a honor student and captain of the football team.

After one year at Dartmouth College, John dropped out to prepare for the AAU National All-Around competition—ten track and field events performed all in one day, like the decathlon. John won the championship in 1908 and posed for a statue they put in Union Station in Washington.

John transferred to Princeton, where he broke his nose as a star halfback on the football team and went on to get a civil engineering degree in 1912.

That summer he went to Celtic Park, Long Island, to defend his AAU All-Around championship against the great Jim Thorpe, who had just finished winning gold medals in the decathlon and the pentathlon in the Summer Olympics in Stockholm.

In the rain and mud at the AAU meet, Bredemus and Thorpe both broke the old records, but Thorpe won by a mere 173 points. In January of 1913 the Olympic Committee and the AAU accused Thorpe of being a professional because he had played semipro baseball in North Carolina in 1909 and 1910.

The controversy over Thorpe's gold medals lingers to this day. I think most people have always wished Thorpe could have kept them or have them returned to him.

Instead his Olympic gold medals were returned to the committee and put into a bank vault. Thorpe's AAU All-Around gold medals were presented to John Bredemus. John accepted the gold medals and kept them until shortly before he died.

In June of 1913 John was named athletic director at Stamford Prep in Connecticut. He worked as a lifeguard at Brighton Beach. That summer he took up golf at Van Cortland Park—America's first public course, built in the Bronx—and by 1914 he was entering tournaments.

In 1915 John put his civil engineering degree to use working for the team that built the Lido Club on Long

Island. He became one of the first golf architects in this country.

The PGA was chartered in 1916 at a meeting at New York's Taplow Club. John was one of the first members. He came to Texas in 1919, looking for a place to play golf year round, and was hired as a high school principal in San Antonio.

Texas's first—and at the time only—public course was Brackenridge Park in San Antonio, where John became a regular and soon was assistant pro. In 1920 John was hired to build San Felipe Springs, which is still an excellent course in Del Rio. He was the first real golf architect in Texas. Before John, golf holes had been laid out by committees or by players, as when Lewis Hancock had walked off the first Austin Country Club nine-hole layout with his friends.

For much of the above information, I am indebted to my friend Francis Trimble of the Texas Golf Hall of Fame in Houston. Now we reach the time I came to know John myself.

It was Bredemus who gave the first lessons in Texas, staged the first Texas tournament, built Corpus Christi Country Club in 1923, and wrote the first golf instructional pieces for Texas newspapers.

Credit for dreaming up and organizing the first Texas Open, won by Bob MacDonald in San Antonio in 1922, usually goes to sportswriter Jack O'Brien of San Antonio. But it was Bredemus who was the genius behind it. The best golfers in the world converged on Texas for that tournament and started a golf boom.

In 1922 the Texas PGA had been formed with Houston Country Club pro Willie Maguire as president and Bredemus as secretary. John advocated a "winter tour." He was on hand for the first Shreveport (La.) Open but when he used bent grass at Colonial, that course became known as the first bent-grass greens in Texas.

While John was building Colonial, he wanted to cut down a huge oak called Big Annie that guarded the 17th green. John would cut down a tree any time if he thought it improved the course in terms of air circulation or sunlight. But Marvin Leonard, whose money was being spent on the project, drove out and stopped Big Annie from being cut down while workers were digging at the roots.

There is a story that John got into a huff and Marvin Leonard fired him. The truth is that John was ill, and he turned the finishing of the course over to his protégé, Ralph Plummer. John told me, "Why should I argue with Mr. Leonard? He's paying the bills."

Many years later a storm destroyed Big Annie.

I think Perry Maxwell was called in to do some cosmetic work at Colonial before the 1941 U.S. Open, but the course is John's design.

One time John took me to the site where he was laying out the second 18 holes at Fort Worth's Ridglea Country Club. He said, "Here will be a tee and over there a green, Harvey." He could picture all the holes in his head. The main thing I could picture was that we were knee deep in brush and I was getting covered by chiggers.

John taught me it takes the eyes of an artist to design a course, but the skills of an engineer to build one. John was both.

John worked on many famous courses in Texas that are credited to others, as well as many that do bear his name, like Braeburn in Houston, the historic Offat's Bayou in Galveston (sadly destroyed to build an Air Force runway during World War II), Memorial Park in

(1922), the first Texas Open (1922), the first Corpus Christi Open (1923), the first Houston Open (1924) and the first Dallas Open (1926).

In 1927 Bredemus landed the National PGA for Cedar Crest in Dallas. To prepare for the tournament he added forty bunkers to the old Tillinghast course and lengthened it several hundred yards.

Golf courses were being built all over the state, and I think John had a hand in about 80 percent of them.

We hired John as our architect at the old Austin Country Club in 1924 when we changed from sand greens to grass. He would drop in every week or so and supervise the construction. There were no bulldozers then. We did the work with mules and heavy scrapers.

When our club moved to Riverside Drive, I asked John to design it. He said, "Harvey, I'm working on two courses right now. I don't think I could do you justice if I took on a third." We brought in Perry Maxwell to do the job. Perry had just had a leg amputated, and he went around on his peg leg as he laid out our course. Perry built some of the finest contour greens I ever saw. They've been changed since.

John traveled with just a few clothes, a bag of books, a canvas golf bag of seven clubs, a checkerboard and a sockful of checkers. John was often seen to beat Titanic Thompson in their checkers matches in Houston. Taking off across the state by himself, telling no one where he was going or what he was working on, John built golf courses without leaving records. He didn't want fame. Nobody knew what he did with the money he was making. He wasn't spending it on himself.

John's most famous course is Colonial Country Club in Fort Worth, built in 1936. Bredemus had put in bentgrass greens in San Angelo in 1928 and Seguin in 1935,

Houston (the best muny in the country at the time), Hermann Park muny in Houston, and others too numerous to name. If he didn't build the course, chances are he came along later and changed it—as when he put in grass greens in place of sand at our Austin Country Club.

He and I were driving back home from Louisiana in the rain one night, and our car got stuck in the mud in Liberty, Texas. John jumped out of the car and shouted, "If this is Liberty, give me death!"

Toward the end of his life John was the head pro at Hermann Park in Houston. He would visit the Burkes at River Oaks and sit under the trees and play checkers with the members. But John wouldn't go into the clubhouse. He said he felt he didn't belong among the people inside.

I asked John what was his favorite of all the sports he played when he was young.

He said, "Harvey, the most fun I ever had was hopping freight cars in my hometown and waving at the people as I passed."

Not long before he died, John showed me Jim Thorpe's gold medals. He kept them in a cigar box.

"You know what I'm going to do with these things at last?" he asked.

"No. What?" I said.

"I think I'm going to melt them down," he said.

That's what I think happened to Jim Thorpe's gold medals.

Hooking and Slicing

HOOKS DON'T HURT the average golfer. It's the pulled hook that does the damage. If the average golfer is hitting a shot that flies straight and hooks toward the end, don't worry about it.

If your ball starts immediately to the left, and then hooks, you need help from a pro.

The first place to look is your grip. Take the privilege of making the V's of one or both hands point at your chin.

When one cures a hook by putting the left hand too much on top of the club, it is only a matter of time before the swing gets out and over the ball.

In your swing, concentrate on clipping the tee or brushing the grass. This will take the club straight through.

Opening the face of your club a little at address is practically the same thing as weakening your grip.

The slicer has a much worse time of it than the hooker.

Many high-handicappers hit a slice as such a regular thing that they allow for it when they take aim. If you allow for a slice, you are almost certainly going to get one. (Allowing for a hook is also conducive to hooking.)

The slicer should first hold the club lightly and look to the grip.

You have the privilege to make your V's of either or both hands point to your right shoulder.

Again, clip the tee or brush the grass to make your clubface go straight through. Make sure to hold the club lightly. Think of it as a fine musical instrument. You wouldn't try to play a clarinet by crushing it, would you? Hold it lightly all the way through the swing.

A sure cure for the slicer is to pretend you are on a baseball field at home plate. Take your stance to aim your body slightly to the right of second base, but aim your clubface straight at the base. Then hit the ball over the shortstop. Use a 7-iron at first, then a 3-wood.

Be careful the downswing is not from the outside. Come down the line on plane and hit a hard fly ball over the shortstop, using primarily the left forearm and possibly rotating the whole left arm. This is the best cure for slicing that I know.

Read this carefully and I'm sure you can hook the ball.

Strange Penalty

THE MOST EMBARRASSING thing you can do in golf is swing your driver on the tee and completely miss the ball.

For this humiliation, the penalty is one stroke.

However, if you smash a drive a long way but the ball lands an inch out of bounds, the penalty is stroke and distance—in effect, a two-shot punishment for what was nearly a good drive.

Yardage

WHEN THE U.S. Open was held at Colonial in 1941, I noticed they had taken out some trees at the 150-yard markers. So I wrote the USGA and asked them about it. I was figuring on planting trees at Austin Country Club. The USGA wrote back and said that to plant trees at the 150-yard markers was not illegal, but no USGA tournament would be played on a course that used them.

Instead of trees at Austin Country Club, I put pipes and white sticks in the ground at 150 yards. These could be removed for a tournament. Even at that, I was accused of giving our home players an advantage over visitors.

Now on the professional tour a player knows the yardage down to the foot on every shot. They even give the pros a sheet of paper showing exactly where the pin is on each green.

The confidence they receive from knowing the exact yardage is a great help.

Most country clubs and good municipal courses today have trees or bushes at the 150-yard and 100-yard markers and frequently paint the yardage on sprinkler heads.

We used to judge the yardage by eye and feel.

Ben Hogan was uncanny at it.

Making an episode of the TV show *Shell's Wonderful World of Golf,* Ben looked at the scorecard on a par-three hole. The card said it was 152 yards to the center of the green. "This card is wrong," Ben said. "It's 148 yards to the middle."

They measured it, and Ben was right.

Tom Kite has a wonderful sense for distance.

Many pros send their caddies out to step off the yardage to the green from certain trees or bunkers. I believe Dean Beman, now the PGA Commissioner, started this practice when he was a player, and Jack Nicklaus brought it to a fine art.

Long and Short

Jack Burke, Jr., and I were giving a clinic and somebody asked about shooting at the flag with a long iron.

"I shoot at the middle of the green on long irons," Jack said. "Sometimes the ball rolls up by the flag and makes me look good."

Anybody who can play golf very well can shoot at the flag from 150 yards if the greens are soft. When the course is dry, most players will try to hit the ball too far off the tee and will wind up where they can't play to the pin.

There's no reason why the average golfer should take more than three to get down from 150 yards. If you spend most of your full-swing practice on your 7-, 6- or 5-iron—whichever is your 150-yard shot—you will develop the confidence to hit the middle of the green, and maybe it will roll close to the cup and make you look good.

Best Dressed

I THINK THE three best-dressed male golfers I ever saw were Walter Hagen, Horton Smith and Ben Hogan. They had style and class in my opinion.

Jimmy Demaret became noted for his colorful attire, which looked good on Jimmy but not on the people who copied him.

Hogan dressed in light and dark and always looked good in photographs. Hagen and Smith wore neckties, long-sleeve dress shirts and knickers. Their clothes were neatly pressed. The Great Depression put knickers out of business. People couldn't afford to pay $12 for a good pair of wool hose to wear with them. They needed to buy a pair of long pants.

Hogan used to start off a merchandising speech wearing rumpled clothes. Halfway through the talk, he would leave the stage, only to reappear in elegantly conservative attire.

"Who'd you rather buy from—that first guy or me?" Ben would ask.

Professional golfers are out there to put on a show for the public. I think they should set an example of tasteful dress, but I suppose I'm hopelessly old-fashioned.

I think the women are dressing better than the men.

My Best Boys

I COUNT MY BLESSINGS that I have taught and coached, as youngsters of school age, four truly great male players.

I wouldn't try to compare them as to who I thought was best. All four are great in their own way.

They are:

Ed White, who had a distinguished amateur career. He beat Fred Haas, Jr., in the finals of the NCAA at Congressional Country Club in Washington, D.C. Fred told me Ed was the best player he ever saw. Ed never turned pro. There wasn't enough money on the tour in those days to suit Ed.

Morris Williams, Jr., killed in a plane crash just as he was about to start on the tour. I had to relay the tragic information to his mother and his father, who was the sports editor of the Austin paper. His daddy fainted in my arms.

Tom Kite, golf's all-time leading money winner.

Ben Crenshaw, Masters champion.

Another of my special boys was the late Davis Love, Jr. He came to me for coaching at age 17 and played four years at the University of Texas. Davis was good enough to qualify for the Masters as an undergraduate. But Davis, a keen student of the game, never wanted to play the tour. He wanted to teach—and he became one of the best. His son, Davis Love III, a top tour player, has come to me for a few lessons, but I couldn't improve on his father's instruction.

Chip or Pitch?

ALWAYS CHIP THE ball if:

1. The lie is poor.
2. The green is hard.
3. You have a downhill lie.
4. The wind has an influence on the shot.
5. You are under stress.

Probably you want to pitch the ball if:

1. The lie is good.
2. You have an uphill lie.
3. The green is very soft.
4. There is an obstacle in the way.

Ability must be considered. The expert player can play a delicate chip with a sand wedge that would be very risky for a high handicapper. These are general guidelines.

A common fault in pitching is for the player to pull up off the shot. This is because the clubhead gets ahead of the hands. To cure this, I will have a student practice hitting a low pitch, as if he wants to hit a shot that would go under a card table. This encourages the student to stay down with the ball and let the loft on the clubhead do the pitching.

Hitting a pitch shot with a sand wedge from any distance, use the full length of the club. Gripping down on a sand wedge is conducive to chili-dipping, which is dropping your head and bending your left arm at impact, causing you to hit behind the ball or else top it.

Never let the clubhead pass your hands on the follow-through of a chip or a short pitch.

There is an important wedge shot to learn for close lies and winter fairways when the grass is dormant. Play the ball off the right foot. Close the blade until it is square to the line and the bounce of the blade does not touch the ground. Adjust your stance forward to compensate for direction. Put slightly more weight on the left foot. Strike the ball and the ground at the same time on the downswing.

This will produce a lower ball with more backspin. It is not a trick shot. It's a shot that comes in handy.

I taught this shot to one of my favorite students, former state senior champion Bill Penn.

He came in and complained, "Harvey, I want a shot that works 100 percent of the time. This one only works three out of four times for me. I two-putted once."

Out of Sight

As I GET OLDER I must be becoming a better teacher.

This must be true, because more of my pupils have started hitting the ball out of my sight.

Or could it be my eyes are fading?

The Follow-through

IN AN EFFORT to have a student learn the right type of action down in the hitting area, one of the first things I do is put him or her in a good follow-through position.

This is important because the follow-through is a reflection of what has gone on before it.

Pictures show the ball is gone from the clubface a fraction of a second after you hit it. So you don't hit it with your follow-through. But if you have made a proper swing, your follow-through will display it.

On the practice line, I will have students pose for a few seconds at the end of the swing in order to study the follow-through. I make sure the follow-through we are studying has been a true result of the swing. An artificial follow-through tells the student nothing.

A balanced follow-through with all the weight on the left foot and the elbows out front of the body is what we want to pose and remember.

Posing after a good shot is fine on the range. Enjoy it. Get into your mind how it feels.

But I don't care for posing on the golf course.

If you hit a good shot but fall back a little or don't quite hold your balance, that's all right on the golf course. You're not getting points for style on the course. Your object is to hit the ball to your target.

If you hit a good shot on the course and wind up in a lovely finish, just bring it down and go on and tend to your business.

A Little Bit

THE GOLF SWING is one swing, but it is made up of little things all working together.

Dutch Harrison said, "A little bit is a little bit."

This means that the club hitting the ball just a little bit off angle is going to grow into a large error by the time the ball flies out there. If the clubface is two or three degrees off at impact, the ball will be 20–30 yards off at 200 yards.

There are four things that make a good shot—angle of clubface, path of club, clubhead speed at impact and hitting the ball in the center of the clubface.

We talk so much about the swing that we forget the angle of face at impact is just as important.

Many golfers look at the so-called slice slashes on the bottoms of their woods and think they are swinging across the ball from the outside.

But it could just as easily be an open clubface that causes the marks.

Square your clubface at address to give yourself a better chance to keep it square at impact. Some students insist on opening their clubface at address, and a very few feel better with it closed. When I show them a square clubface, they can hardly believe it.

There is no other feeling quite like the euphoria of hitting a golf ball with a square clubface and connecting on what is called the sweet spot. Actually the sweet spot is the "no-roll" spot, where the ball comes off absolutely straight, not spinning to one side or the other. This shot is usually hit accidentally, even though you are trying.

The average player will hit maybe three shots on the sweet spot in 18 holes. Ben Hogan said by his high standards he hit the sweet spot maybe once in a round. "If I hit the sweet spot four or five times, I would shoot in the fifties," he told me.

The important question is not how good your good shots are—it's how bad are your bad ones?

Even beginners hit one of these sweet-spot shots now and then. The rush of thrill and excitement resulting from it is what inspires learners to want to get better, so they can have this wondrous feeling again.

One does not try to square the clubface. It just gets squared up in a good swing.

Players readily admit, "I'm a golf nut," or "I'm a golf addict."

They get addicted to the joy of hitting good shots.

When you begin to square your clubface, you will satisfy your addiction much more often.

Remember—a little bit is a little bit.

A Golfer's Poem

TIMES HAVE NOT changed! Dorothy Bible, whose noted husband, D. X., was football coach and athletic director at the University of Texas and one of the wildest drivers of the golf ball I ever saw, sent the following gem clipped from the Lincoln, Nebraska, *Star* and dated Thursday, June 19, 1930:

COMFORTLESS
by Edgar A. Guest

I found him underneath a tree
  "And what is wrong," quoth I,
"That you so solemn seem to be
  Under this summer sky?

"The birds above you gayly sing,
  The wildflowers brightly bloom,
What is this awful, horrid thing
  Which seems to seal your doom?

"Round you the children romp and play,
  The gentle breezes blow.
Sad stranger, tell to me I pray
  The burden of your woe."

"I do not see the sunbeams dance,
  Nor hear the birds," said he.
"There's something faulty with my stance,
  I can't get off the tee.

"All day I've shanked my mashie shot,
  My putts rimmed every cup,
I'm doing something I should not;
  I think it's looking up."

"Poor man," I said, " 'tis very sure
  No help for you appears,
The woes you bear I tried to cure
  Myself for thirty years.

"And still my mashie shots I shank,
  And still I slice the drive,
And with the dubs expect to rank
  As long as I'm alive.

"Through time all other griefs may cure,
  All other hurts may mend,
The miseries of golf endure:
  To them there is no end."

Preparing for a Big Match

BE YOURSELF. Do as you usually do. If you ordinarily have a couple of drinks in the evening, do it. If you have been going to bed at 11 P.M., do not crawl between the sheets two hours earlier than normal. Eat the same food you usually eat, and at the same hour.

You must understand that it is your mind that will have the most to do with how you play in the big match.

That's why you should avoid new or different things that will distract your mind from your normal routine.

Put the results of the big match out of your thoughts. The results are in the future. You want to stay in the present.

At the course before the big match, warm up as usual. If you ordinarily put on your shoes, hit half a dozen balls and go to the tee, keep it the same. Hitting a whole bag of balls will only hurt you, unless you always warm up with a whole bag.

This is no time to make a change in your swing or your grip. You must "dance with what brung you."

When you go to the first tee, don't even consider the eventual result of the round. Consider the shot at hand. Sandra Haynie, an LPGA Hall of Famer who grew up in

Austin and Fort Worth would not watch her opponents hit their shots. I don't necessarily recommend this for everyone, but it may help you stay concentrated on your own shot.

Try and play each shot to the best of your ability, one shot at a time—and *take dead aim!*

Uphill and Downhill

WITH AN UPHILL lie, you are going to pull the ball. Go ahead and make allowance for it.

Shorten your uphill leg and straighten the other, so that your hips are level. You will naturally play the ball back in your stance, but don't let your weight shift back with it.

On a downhill lie, straighten your downhill leg and flex the uphill leg, again to level the hips. Play the ball back toward your right foot. Sole your club on the ground and the manufacturer will tell you about where it belongs when the face is square.

You may hit the ball a little to the right. But do not play for a slice off a downhill lie. If you do, you are in danger of shanking it.

Playing in the Wind

MY OLD FRIEND Jimmie Connolly, a fine player, used to have trouble playing in the wind. The night before he played a 36-hole match in high wind for the Texas Amateur Championship, he asked me for advice. This is what I told him:

Wind tends to make people hurry. I believe more accidents happen on and off the golf course in March than any other month, because of the wind.

On all shots in the wind, including the putter, pay careful attention to your balance. Do not hurry yourself or your swing. Just be normal. With a driver, tee the ball a little lower against the wind and a little higher when the wind is with you.

Scratch players or pros can hit the old Demaret Quail Shot into the wind, but I don't recommend this shot for the average player. It requires precise timing and a great deal of practice.

Instead, I say if your shot calls for a 5-iron on an ordinary day, into the wind you should hit a 4-iron, or even a 3-iron. The loft on the club will keep the ball low.

If the wind is helping on the same shot, choose a 6-iron, 7-iron, or even an 8-iron.

Remember, the wind is blowing as hard for your opponent as it is for you. Take your time. Keep your balance. Don't let the wind make you hurry or swing hard.

Jimmie Connolly won the state title the next day, 5 and 4.

Titanic Thompson

Austin is an easy drive from Fort Worth, Dallas, San Antonio and Houston, so naturally our town became a place for traveling hustlers to pause for some action.

Ben Hogan told me about a man named Alvin C. Thomas, later famous as Titanic Thompson, who was hustling in Fort Worth. "He's bound to come through Austin and want to play," Ben said. "He can play left-handed or right-handed, and you can't beat him."

Sure enough, one Sunday afternoon things had slowed down and I was sitting in the golf shop when a stranger walked in and introduced himself. "I am Herman Kaiser from Ardmore, Oklahoma." He showed me his PGA card and asked if he could play our course.

I said that was fine. Kaiser pointed to a big, handsome fellow and said, "This is my amateur friend, Mr. Thomas, a member of my club." As Kaiser and his friend started out the door, Thomas said, "Would you like to play with us?" I said no, I guess not.

They went out on the front nine. One of our members who liked playing for a lot of money came in. I told him about Thomas. The member said, "Harvey, let's catch them on the back side and play them. We'll beat them out of a few hundred. I'll pay if we lose."

So I was out practicing when Thomas and his friend came through. Thomas sat down on a bench. He was wearing a pair of cord shoes, not spikes. I said we'd like to play. Thomas said, "We'll play you all for a dollar a hole, or ten, a hundred, a thousand, you name it." He let us see there was a hole in the sole of his shoe.

I said I'd start off playing the back nine for fifty dollars each, which was a lot of money to me.

We began playing. On the third hole, five or six men in street clothes showed up. They had been playing poker in the clubhouse and came out to see us play golf. Titanic flashed a roll of hundred-dollar bills, and asked if I thought they wanted his money.

On about the sixth hole, Thomas said, "I sure like this place. I think I may stay around for a while." This was shortly before Christmas. Thomas pulled out a little brown candy bag. "You want to give your wife something nice for Christmas?" he said. "Give her a few of these."

The bag was full of diamonds.

I said, no thanks, I guess not.

By the last hole, Thomas and his partner had holed a couple of long putts and beat us one-up.

In the golf shop afterward, Thomas bought fifty dollars worth of stuff to make up for what I had lost. "I was really lucky today," he told me, the way a hustler would. "You guys nearly had us."

A few months later I saw a picture in the paper of Thomas's partner.

Herman Kaiser's picture was in the paper because he had just won the Masters.

We had many hustlers pass through town.

One big fellow who claimed to be an Indian wanted to play with me using my clubs and him using a slingshot. I took him on. He was very accurate from short range, but he couldn't shoot the ball far enough from the tee with his slingshot to beat me.

Maybe the most bizarre hustlers we ever had were the Duke of Paducah and the Masked Marvel. The Duke was selling tickets for a big match of the Masked Marvel against the strongest challenger in town. They decided they wanted to play me for "charity."

We found out why the Marvel wore a mask.

He and the Duke intended to steal the ticket money and escape before the match. We checked up on them and then called off the game and urged them to leave Austin.

Another hustler was hanging around our club trying to get a match when Wilmer Allison walked up and said, "Anybody want to putt against me?"

The hustler's eyes lit up.

"I do," the hustler said. "How much do you want to play for?"

Wilmer said, "The usual—twenty-five cents."

The hustler grabbed his bag and departed to the sound of our laughter.

Trick Shots

HITTING TRICK SHOTS is a dying art.

Back in the 1920's and 1930's golf was thought of as an elite game for the wealthy, and baseball was the game for plain folks. This was long before Arnold Palmer came along and made golf a game for everybody.

But in the old days, a golf pro who needed a few extra dollars would do well to learn trick shots and put on exhibitions.

I gave an exhibition one day between games of a baseball doubleheader at the old ball park in Austin. When I walked out to home plate, the crowd took one look at me in my plus-four knickers and plaid socks and started booing.

They quieted down some when I started hitting curves to the right and to the left. Then I placed one ball on top of another with a bit of putty. I hit the bottom ball 125 yards with a 7-iron, and the top ball popped into the air so I could catch it in my hand. Almost any good player can do this trick, but the people in the stands didn't know that.

I lined up two balls and hit them with one swing—one ball a big hook and the other a big slice. They crossed in midair.

I had a rubber hose, the kind you put air in your car tires with. It had a grip on one end and a 3-wood head on the other. I hit a few shots with that rubber hose, and people started cheering.

I took a left-handed club and hit it right-handed. I pulled out a right-handed club, turned the head upside down, and hit it. This shot looks impossible, but I could spin the club in my fingers so fast nobody could see that the face was hitting the ball square.

I had a device that had a steel ball attached to a piece of chain that was attached to a grip, and I hit some golf balls 100 yards with that.

By the time I started hitting 7-irons over the center field fence, the whole crowd was applauding.

I don't mind admitting the applause sounded a whole lot better than the boos that had greeted me.

Joe Kirkwood was the best trick-shot artist I ever saw. His most astounding trick was one he would do only once at a session. He'd place the ball in a grassy bunker on an uphill lie facing away from the green, make a swing and the ball would go backward over his head and land within 10 feet of the cup.

A company wanted to film a hole-in-one and hired Joe to hit it for them. They wanted the ball to hit past the hole and back into the cup. They brought many reels of film, thinking it might take days. Joe made the hole-in-one from 150 yards on his eighth swing.

There is a monument to Joe on the seventh hole at Brackenridge Park to mark the spot where he curved a ball out of the woods onto the green and won the Texas Open.

People always wondered why a pro who could hit shots like Joe didn't win every tournament. He told me, "Maybe I could—if every shot was a trick shot."

Paul Hahn was another great trick-shot artist who became a friend of mine. He and I played an exhibition match at Austin Country Club, and afterward Paul started doing his trick-shots show. He was working for a whiskey distiller. Paul pointed to a telephone pole 125 yards away and told a French countess in the gallery, Mrs. Tips, that if he missed the pole he would give her a bottle of whiskey. He hit the pole dead center.

Then Paul sent a caddie onto the green 100 yards away and said, "Be ready to pull the pin when I hit this ball into the hole." He turned to the countess, "If it doesn't go in, you get a bottle of whiskey."

His shot landed on the green and rolled up to the hole, but the caddie was so excited he didn't pull the pin in time and the ball hit it.

The old trick-shot artist has been replaced by the long-driving artists now. In my prime I could hardly even show a muscle with my biceps, but these long-driving artists are big, powerful athletes who can hammer the ball 350 yards or more. They have their own long-driving tour.

I miss the trick-shot exhibitions. Hitting a big hook or slice, a low ball or a high ball, was easy for a trick-shot artist because you made it happen with your swing.

The thing you didn't want to hear was someone in the crowd shout, "Now hit a straight one."

A straight ball is the hardest one to hit.

Ben Hogan always said if you hit a straight ball, it was an accident.

Caddies

My mother wouldn't let me caddie until I started school in 1914. My brothers Tom and Tinsley were already caddying. When I was finally old enough, Tom took me to the club. You didn't just walk right into the caddie shack and be accepted. There were a lot of boys looking for bags to carry. You had to earn your place. It was an edge for me to have my big brother Tom as the head caddie, number one, who gave out the badges. Anybody who caused trouble for me or Tinsley, number eleven, would have to whip Tom, which they couldn't do.

Golfers didn't practice so much in the days when they had to pick up their own balls or else hire a caddie for twenty-five cents an hour to stand down on the range with their shag bags. It was dangerous, all those golfers hitting balls and kids out there picking them up. I must have been hit twenty times.

As a caddie, I learned to imitate the swings of every player in the club. For a nickel or a dime, I would put on a show.

Later when I became a pro, I would notice caddies imitating my swing. It was a great way to learn to play golf.

It's rare to find a club that has caddies today. For one thing, if caddies do show up and wait for a bag, the club has to pay the minimum wage even if they're just sitting.

For another, of course, the club makes much more money renting golf carts.

I miss having caddies hanging around the course. They were very colorful characters and added a lot of spirit to the game.

When I was a boy caddies were not allowed to play the course even if they could afford the fifty-cent green fee. But my friend Charlie Clark and I talked Mrs. Reinli, the club manager, into taking our money one Saturday morning, and we teed off.

At the eighth hole our old Scottish pro, Bill MacKenzie, rose up out of a bunker and yelled in his roughest brogue, "What're ye lads doin' here!"

We told him we had paid.

"Go get yer money back and don't let me catch ye out here ever again!" he yelled.

We were happy he didn't fire us.

I was the first head pro I know of who let caddies play the course. They had to play Saturday morning and finish before noon—people worked a five and a half day week in those days—but they could play.

A Life in Golf

I ONCE HEARD a woman ask, "I wonder how Harvey makes a living? All he does is hang around Austin Country Club."

In a roundabout way I have somehow tried to teach each of my students that golf and life are similar. There's nothing guaranteed to be fair in either golf or life, and we shouldn't expect it to be different.

You must accept your disappointments and triumphs equally.

If you're a pro you may go out there and finish second in the big money, and still you will roll and tumble in bed all night, thinking if you had just made a certain putt or two you would have finished first.

One person can put this kind of thinking behind and go on, but the next one can't and continues tossing and turning, suffering in the mind.

To some it doesn't seem fair that Ben Crenshaw can walk onto a course and just naturally play great golf at the age of 12, where others might work all their life and never approach being as good.

I played in a lot of tournaments, but I felt that I was playing as much for what I could learn from my fellow pros as for any chance of winning. I knew I wanted to teach, and this was an important part of my learning.

Golf tells you much about character. Play a round of golf with someone, and you know them more intimately than you might from years of dinner parties.

Just watching how close a player steps to the cup when retrieving the ball reveals whether this is a thoughtful, considerate person.

I took care of golf courses for forty years as the superintendent as well as the pro. I used to fight worms. Worms came up through the greens, aerifying them, and as soon as that dirt goes through a worm it's the best fertilizer that could be. But too many worms means too much fertilizer. So we spread a little lye on the greens, turned on the sprinkler and the worms came tumbling out. We would whip the worms down with a pole and scrape them up with an early-bird rake. We didn't have pesticides. Worms were fine up to a certain point.

We used a spade fork to mash down until you hear the grass pop, aerifying. We would take two men and spend four or five days working from the first to the eighteenth green in the early spring.

Some places put bird boxes around the greens and encouraged birds to move in. When we saw a lot of birds on the greens, we knew we had an insect problem.

When I took the pro job in 1923, Austin Country Club—which was chartered in 1898 as one of the first two golf clubs in Texas—was a sand greens course, as were most courses in the state. We had nine holes until March 2, 1914.

The term "tee box" comes from the box of sand that used to stand at the driving-off places. Players would use the sand to build up little mounds, or tees, to hit the ball off.

In 1924 I convinced the Board to put in grass greens. Austin Muny, where my brother Tom later became the pro, was putting in Bermuda-grass greens, and I argued that we needed them, too.

When we moved the course to Riverside Drive, our

architect, Perry Maxwell, put in bent-grass greens. Then we moved to our Pete Dye course in the hills along the lake. I've worn out three courses.

In the old days when they started fertilizing their fairways at Dallas Country Club, Al Badger went over to Fort Worth and got all the cow manure they had at the stockyards. He spread cow manure all over the fairways. This stuff really stunk. Dallas Country Club is in Highland Park, a very ritzy neighborhood. Poor Al took a lot of abuse for that.

If he had used rabbit manure, there wouldn't have been a smell. But how could he have caught enough rabbits, or raided enough hutches, to cover every fairway? Highland Park smelled like cow manure for months.

When they tore down the old courthouse in Austin, they found bat guano three feet deep in the attic. I got an old truck and brought that precious fertilizer back to Austin Country Club. As we drove by the high school in our truck, we passed my daughter, Kathryn, walking home with friends. She pretended not to know me.

I have watched Austin Country Club grow from a nine-hole sand greens course into one of the prettiest, most challenging courses in the country. We have the Colorado River, lakes, canyons, creeks, trees, wild flowers, deer, rabbits, squirrels, birds everywhere.

At first I thought our Pete Dye design might be too difficult for our members. But as our course has matured, our members on all levels of ability have learned to love it as I do. With four tees to each hole, any realistic player can enjoy the game here.

I feel that good bent-grass greens like ours are superior to good Bermuda-grass greens.

If somebody came to me and said, "Harvey, if you had

started as a banker when you were a young man, by now you'd be a wealthy retired bank president. Wouldn't that be better than being a retired grownup caddie?"

If they had said that, and they did, I would answer, "When I was a young man, you didn't become president of a bank unless you were a member of the family that owned it. My oldest brother, Fred, a teller, was the oldest employee of the American Bank. Fred was perfectly satisfied and happy and retired to a two-story home by Onion Creek. But with my ability and my schooling there was no profession anywhere that suited me as much as golf."

The best part of golf is that if you observe the etiquette, you can always find a game. I don't care how good you play, you can find somebody who can beat you, and I don't care how bad you play, you can find somebody you can beat.

The most important thing I can say to any young man or woman who is contemplating a life in golf is this: marry a good person like I did.

Thank you, Helen.